TOM STOPPARD

MODERN LITERATURE SERIES

GENERAL EDITOR: Philip Winsor

In the same series:

(continued on last page of book)

TOM STOPPARD

Felicia Hardison Londré

FREDERICK UNGAR PUBLISHING CO.
NEW YORK

For Patricia McIlrath

Copyright© 1981 by Frederick Ungar Publishing Co.
Printed in the United States of America
Design by Anita Duncan

Library of Congress Cataloging in Publication Data

Londré, Felicia Hardison, 1941-
    Tom Stoppard.

    (Modern literature monographs)
    Bibliography: p.
    Includes index.
    1.   Stoppard, Tom—Criticism and interpretation.
PR6069.T6Z75   822'.914   80-53698
ISBN 0-8044-2538-8

Contents

Chronology

1937	JULY 3. Tom Stoppard is born Tomas Straussler in Zlín, Czechoslovakia, the second son of Dr. and Mrs. Eugene Straussler.
1939	The family moves to Singapore.
1942	Mrs. Straussler and her sons are evacuated to Darjeeling, India, where Tom attends an American-run multilingual school. Dr. Straussler is killed during the Japanese invasion of Singapore.
1945–1946	Martha Straussler marries Kenneth Stoppard, a British Army major stationed in India. After the war, the family moves to England.
1946–1954	Stoppard attends Dolphin School in Nottinghamshire and Pocklington School in Yorkshire.
1954	Stoppard becomes a junior general reporter for the *Western Daily Press*. He reviews plays and makes friends at the Bristol Old Vic.
1958	He is hired as a reporter and feature writer at the *Bristol Evening World*.
1960	JULY. He resigns from his newspaper job and supports himself by free-lancing while he writes plays. Kenneth Ewing becomes his agent. *A Walk on the Water* is optioned by H.M. Tennent, but not produced.

1962   He moves to London and becomes drama critic
            for *Scene* magazine for the eight months of its
            existence.

1963   NOVEMBER.   *A Walk on the Water* is produced
            on British Independent Television.

1964   FEBRUARY 20.   *The Dissolution of Dominic
            Boot* is broadcast on BBC Radio.

            APRIL 6.   *M is for Moon Among Other
            Things* is broadcast on BBC Radio.

            MAY–OCTOBER.   Stoppard participates in
            a colloquium in Berlin, sponsored by the Ford
            Foundation, for young playwrights. He writes a
            one-act verse burlesque entitled *Rosencrantz
            and Guildenstern Meet King Lear*. *A Walk on
            the Water* is produced in Hamburg.

            Three of Stoppard's short stories are pub-
            lished by Faber and Faber in *Introduction 2:
            Stories by New Writers*.

1965   He marries Jose Ingle.

            The Gamblers is produced by the Drama
            Department at Bristol University.

            Stoppard writes seventy episodes of *A
            Student's Diary*, a serial about an Arab in Lon-
            don, translated into Arabic and broadcast on
            BBC Radio. *A Walk on the Water* is broadcast on
            BBC Radio in November 1965.

1966   FEBRUARY 8.   *If You're Glad I'll Be Frank* is
            broadcast on BBC Radio.

            MAY 25.   Stoppard's adaptation of *Tango*
            by Slawomir Mrozek is produced by the Royal
            Shakespeare Company.

            AUGUST.   *Rosencrantz and Guildenstern
            Are Dead* is produced by the Oxford Theatre
            Group on the Fringe of the Edinburgh Festival.
            Lord Malquist and Mr Moon is published.

            AUGUST 22.   *A Separate Peace* is produced
            on BBC Television.

1967   FEBRUARY 7.   *Teeth* is produced on BBC Tele-
            vision.

APRIL 11. *Rosencrantz and Guildenstern Are Dead* is produced by the National Theatre at the Old Vic. Stoppard wins the John Whiting Award from the Arts Council of Great Britain and (jointly with David Storey) the *Evening Standard* Award for Most Promising Playwright. The play is revived in London in 1973 and in 1979.

JUNE 28. *Another Moon Called Earth* is produced on BBC Television.

JULY 13. *Albert's Bridge* is broadcast on BBC Radio. It wins the Prix Italia.

OCTOBER 16. *Rosencrantz and Guildenstern Are Dead* opens in New York. It wins the Antoinette Perry (Tony) Award and the Drama Critics Circle Award for Best Play of 1967–1968.

1968   MARCH 28. *Enter A Free Man* (a revised version of *A Walk on the Water*) is produced in London.

JUNE 17. *The Real Inspector Hound* opens in London.

DECEMBER 11. *Neutral Ground* is produced on Granada Television.

1969   AUGUST 29. *Albert's Bridge* and *If You're Glad I'll Be Frank*, two radio plays, are staged on the Fringe of the Edinburgh Festival.

1970   JANUARY 28. *Where Are They Now?* is broadcast on BBC Radio.

MARCH 8. *The Engagement* is broadcast on NBC Television.

APRIL 9. *After Magritte* is produced in London by Inter-Action at the Green Banana Restaurant.

1971   DECEMBER 7. *Dogg's Our Pet* is produced in London by Inter-Action at the Almost Free Theatre.

He is divorced from Jose Ingle.

1972   FEBRUARY 2. *Jumpers* is produced by the National Theatre at the Old Vic. It wins the

Evening Standard Award and the *Plays and Players* Award for Best Play of the year. It opens in New York on April 22, 1974. It is revived at the National Theatre in London in 1976.

FEBRUARY 11. Stoppard marries Dr. Miriam Moore-Robinson, medical director of Syntex Pharmaceuticals.

APRIL. *After Magritte* and *The Real Inspector Hound* are produced on a double bill in London. They open in New York on April 23.

NOVEMBER 14. *Artist Descending A Staircase* is broadcast on BBC Radio.

1973   MARCH 22. Stoppard's English version of *The House of Bernarda Alba* by Federico García Lorca is produced in London.

APRIL 18. *Born Yesterday* by Garson Kanin opens, directed by Stoppard.

1974   JUNE 10. *Travesties* is produced by the Royal Shakespeare Company. It opens in New York on October 30, 1975.

1975   Stoppard writes *Boundaries,* a television play in a series, with Clive Exton.

Stoppard writes the screenplay adaptation of Thomas Wiseman's novel *The Romantic Englishwoman.*

APRIL. *Dirty Linen* and *New-Found-Land* are produced by Inter-Action. The production moves to the Arts Theatre in June. It opens in New York on January 11, 1977.

AUGUST 24. Stoppard's *The (15 Minute) Dogg's Troupe Hamlet* is performed by Inter-Action on the terraces of the National Theatre in London.

AUGUST. Stoppard, a member of the Committee Against Psychiatric Abuse, addresses a rally in Trafalgar Square and participates in a march to the Soviet Embassy, to deliver a petition on the rights of Soviet dissidents.

DECEMBER. Stoppard adapts Jerome K. Jerome's novel *Three Men in a Boat* for BBC Television.

1977 FEBRUARY 7. *The Times* prints a letter written by Stoppard, one of the four British members of the International Committee for the Support of the Principles of Charter 77, expressing concern over Czechoslovakian government harassment of Czech playwright Václav Havel.

FEBRUARY. Stoppard visits Moscow and Leningrad with the assistant director of the British section of Amnesty International.

JUNE 18. Stoppard goes to Czechoslovakia, where he meets dissident playwrights Vaclav Havél and Pavel Kohout.

JULY 1. *Every Good Boy Deserves Favour* is produced by the Royal Shakespeare Company with the 100-piece London Symphony Orchestra, conducted by composer André Previn, at the Royal Festival Hall in London for one performance only. Recast and reduced to a 32-piece orchestra, it has an extended run at the Mermaid Theatre in London. It is produced in New York with an 81-piece orchestra at the Metropolitan Opera House July 30 to August 4, 1979.

SEPTEMBER. *Professional Foul* is produced on BBC Television. It wins the British Television Critics' award as the best play of 1977. It is produced by WNET Television in New York in April 1978.

DECEMBER. Stoppard is made Commander of the British Empire.

1978 NOVEMBER 8. *Night and Day* opens in London, It opens in New York on November 27, 1979.

Stoppard writes the screenplay for *Despair*, a film based upon the novel by Vladimir Nabokov.

1979   JUNE 20. *Undiscovered Country,* Stoppard's
                English version of *Das Weite Land* by Arthur
                Schnitzler, opens in London.

                JULY 16. *Dogg's Hamlet, Cahoot's Macbeth* opens in London, produced by the British
                American Repertory Company, directed by Ed
                Berman. It opens in New York on October 3,
                1979.

                Stoppard wins the Hamburg Shakespeare
                Prize for 1979.

                Stoppard writes the screenplay for *The
                Human Factor,* based upon the novel by
                Graham Greene.

1

Visitor Playing the Field

"You have to be foreign to write English with that kind of hypnotized brilliance," one of Tom Stoppard's directors said of his plays.[1] He might have added that one needs to be foreign-born to seem as thoroughly English in manners and temperament as Stoppard, whose patriotic enthusiasm for his adopted country is matched only by the sheer delight with which he uses his adopted language.

A sparkling interplay of puns, literary allusions and in-jokes, and tricks with rhythm and rhyme is the most characteristic feature of Stoppard's work, and it gives the impression that he is quite at home writing in English. He acquired this ability by devoting most of his life, since the age of six, to the voracious reading of books of every kind. Stoppard aligns himself with writers like Vladimir Nabokov and Samuel Beckett, who perfected their styles by writing in a second language. He has said that "it is possibly of significance that I missed the first four years of speaking English."[2]

Stoppard's first language was Czech. He was born Tomas Straussler, on July 3, 1937, in Zlín (renamed Gottwaldov in 1948), Czechoslovakia. His father, Eugene Straussler, was a company doctor for Bata shoe manufacturers. Because of the family's Jewish strain, the doctor, his wife Martha, and their two sons were transferred in 1939, on the eve of the Nazi invasion of

Czechoslovakia, to Singapore. There Stoppard briefly attended an English convent school. When the Japanese invaded Singapore in 1942, women and children were evacuated to India. Dr. Straussler remained behind and was killed.

In Darjeeling, Stoppard was sent to an American-run multiracial boarding school. His mother worked as manageress of a Bata shoe shop and, late in 1945, re-married. Both boys assumed the surname of their step-father, Kenneth Stoppard, a major in the British Army. After the war, Major Stoppard brought the family back with him to England. His work in the machine-tool business necessitated the family's moving from place to place, until they finally settled in Bristol in 1950. Stoppard's brother is now a professional accountant, who manages the dramatist's financial affairs.

Most of Stoppard's formal education was gained at the Dolphin School—a prep school in Not-tinghamshire—and at a public grammar school in Pocklington, Yorkshire. He enjoyed being lionized by classmates for his "Czecho-Chinese-American accent,"[3] but became "bored by the idea of anything intellectual."[4] At seventeen he left school and sold all his Greek and Latin classics.

Stoppard had romantic notions about journalism. When Bristol's *Western Daily Press* hired him as a junior reporter in 1954, he believed he was on his way to becoming a globe-trotting newspaperman, who would type out his stories under a hail of machine-gun bullets. Instead, he lived with his parents and settled for "the glamour of flashing a press card at flower shows."[5] By his second year on the newspaper, he was writing feature stories. He has described the work as "indefatigably facetious. There is a sort of second-rate journalism that presents the journalist more than the subject. I did that."[6]

In 1958 Stoppard moved to a job at the *Bristol Evening World* as feature writer, humor columnist, and second-string drama critic. He made friends among the members of the Bristol Old Vic, the outstanding British regional repertory company at the time. The inspired performances during that season of Peter O'Toole, then relatively unknown, may have served to focus Stoppard's interest on the theatre. Another friend was John Boorman, who later directed the film *Deliverance*. Boorman made a television documentary in which Stoppard performed a surrealist bit of business not unlike the kind of visual jokes he would later use in *After Magritte*.

Stoppard gained a certain celebrity in Bristol for a brand of journalism that strained too hard to be funny and for his eccentric aura—a sophisticated wit undercut by a lack of taste in clothes. The comings and goings of the tall, lanky figure in a mackintosh were "reported as if he were Orson Welles."[7] He later recalled that he was "an awful critic. I operated on the assumption that there was an absolute scale of values against which art could be measured. I didn't trust my own subjective responses. And I never had the moral character to pan a friend. I'll rephrase that. I had the moral character never to pan a friend."[8]

On his twenty-third birthday, while vacationing on Capri, Stoppard decided that he had to make his own opportunity to write and publish outside the journalistic market. He returned to Bristol and quit his regular job, but contracted to write two columns a week to support himself. Panic-stricken at being two years behind schedule with what he had wanted to accomplish before the age of twenty-one, Stoppard wrote his first full-length play, *A Walk on the Water*, in only three months.

When asked why he chose to write plays rather than novels or poetry, Stoppard cites the historical moment. In May 1956, John Osborne's *Look Back in Anger* opened in the West End (London's equivalent of Broadway) and marked a turning point in British theatre. What followed has been described as a theater for writers rather than a theater of commerce, a youthful rather than a middle-aged theater, a theater with scenes set in the kitchen rather than in the drawing room.

John Osborne was only the first of a whole crop of "angry young men" whose plays were successfully produced in the next decade. Playwrights Arnold Wesker, Lindsay Anderson, John Arden, Shelagh Delaney, Ann Jellicoe, and Robert Bolt, and director Joan Littlewood brought to British theatre a vigorous new realism of language and a fresh, nonjudgmental social awareness. Stoppard recalls that "in England at that time seven out of ten who wanted to write were writing plays and the other three were trying. Of these, four would be carbon copies of *Look Back in Anger*, and the other three of *Waiting for Godot*."[9] "Pinter, Osborne, Arden, and Wesker were the four hoarse men of the new apocalypse."[10]

Stoppard acknowledges the influence of Robert Bolt's *Flowering Cherry* and of Arthur Miller on his own *Walk on the Water*, which he has since nicknamed "Flowering Death of a Cherry Salesman." He took it to the Bristol Old Vic for an assessment and heard nothing more of it until nine months—that is, seventy-two newspaper columns—later. In the meantime he wrote a one-act play, *The Gamblers*, which he has since dubbed "Waiting for Godot in the Condemned Cell," to acknowledge the influence of Samuel Beckett's *Waiting for Godot*. Thus, Stoppard's earliest plays substantiate his belief that a first play "tends to be the sum of all the plays you have seen of a type you can emulate technically and have admired."[11]

Someone at the Bristol Old Vic recommended Kenneth Ewing as an agent. Stoppard sent *The Gamblers* to Ewing, who asked if the would-be playwright had anything else. "With misgivings and deprecating noises," says Stoppard, "I sent him *A Walk on the Water*, explaining that it was, or course, rather *passé* compared to the one-acter."[12] Within the week, Stoppard had received "one of those Hollywood-style telegrams that change struggling young artists' lives."[13]

An option on *A Walk on the Water* was picked up by H.M. Tennent, one of Britain's most prestigious producing agencies. With his windfall of a hundred pounds, Stoppard bought twenty books and a Picasso print. He recalls discussions of the play's being done by "various actors, all of whom were knighted."[14] "Because it was not unlike *Flowering Cherry* it was sent to Ralph Richardson, who declined it on the grounds that it was not unlike *Flowering Cherry*."[15] The option ran out at the end of the year and was not renewed.

Three years after it was written, *A Walk on the Water* was finally produced in an adapted version, hastily substituted by British Independent Television, in late November 1963, for another play that was inappropriate so soon after the assassination of President Kennedy. It became Stoppard's first theatrical production when it was staged in Hamburg in 1964 under the name of, *The Spleen of Riley*. After the success of *Rosencrantz and Guildenstern Are Dead*, it was produced in London, much revised, as *Enter A Free Man*, the title of the published version. Although he admits a debt of gratitude and some embarrassed affection for the play, Stoppard agrees with Charles Marowitz's assessment that it is "about as weighty as a feather boa and as substantial as a blancmange left out in the sun."[16] His other journeyman work for the theatre, *The Gamblers*, has been staged only once, by the Drama Department of Bristol University in 1965; it has not been published.

In 1962, Stoppard moved to London, drawn irresistibly to the mecca of British journalism and entertainment. A.C.H. Smith, a fellow journalist from Bristol, remembers that on their trip together Stoppard "had a huge fur coat before men wore them and he sat huddled in it while I was driving my open car to London. He had this slight Czech thing about his 'r' sounds, and he was rolling them, and I suddenly saw this growling bear next to me. He got it and we laughed so much we had to stop."[17] Stoppard may have felt nervous and provincial at first, but he quickly learned his way around Fleet Street, the hub of the London newspaper world.

He had heard that a trendy new show-business magazine was about to be launched. He applied for a staff position and was hired as drama critic. *Scene* magazine began publication in 1963 and, during the next seven months, before it went out of business, Stoppard reviewed 132 shows. Using the pseudonym William Boot, which he borrowed from Evelyn Waugh's novel *Scoop*, Stoppard wrote a number of other pieces for the understaffed magazine.

During that period, Stoppard lived in a dingy one-room apartment, where he spent evenings writing short stories. He abandoned that form after three of them were published by Faber and Faber in 1964. One of his rejected stories became the basis of a fifteen-minute radio play, *'M' Is for Moon Among Other Things*. It was broadcast on BBC Radio in 1964, as was another short piece, *The Dissolution of Dominic Boot*.

Stoppard then wrote a ninety-minute television play, *This Way Out with Samuel Boot*, which his agent Kenneth Ewing offered to one of the commercial television stations. Together they visited the company, only to be told that Stoppard's writing was too "downbeat," that his work was too overscaled for television and that he should "stick to theatre." Driving back from that disappointing meeting (the teleplay has never been produced), they began discussing the Old Vic's production of *Hamlet*. Ewing mentioned an idea he had long cherished: that the King of England who receives

the sealed message ordering the execution of Rosencrantz and Guildenstern might have been King Lear.
Stoppard was attracted to the idea and resolved to write
a play about it.

The opportunity to get back to playwriting came in
the form of a Ford Foundation grant to encourage
young European playwrights, twenty of whom were in-
stalled for five months in a mansion in Berlin. London
critic Charles Marowitz had recommended Stoppard,
who became one of four British grant recipients, along
with James Saunders, Derek Marlowe, and Paul Read.
At the time, Stoppard's track record was perhaps the
least impressive of the four; today, he is the only one
with a truly international reputation.

It was during his Berlin sojourn that *A Walk on the
Water* was produced in Hamburg, and Stoppard
traveled to see it. The theatre had advertised the play
as the work of one of Britain's "angry young men," with
the result that it was the students in the gallery who
were angry at what turned out to be a fairly conventional domestic comedy. They received the play in hostile silence. Afterward, at his German agent's urging,
Stoppard went on stage to take a bow. Borrowing Oscar
Wilde's method of showing indifference to audience
reaction, Stoppard flaunted a cigarette in his mouth. It
was the only time he has been booed off the stage.

One other peripheral activity during the time of
the playwriting grant was his appearance as a cowboy in
a low-budget film made by a Dutch director, based
upon a short story by Jorge Luis Borges. His moment of
glory, twirling a pair of six-shooters in front of the
Brandenberg Gate, has the ring of Stoppard's own
brand of absurdity with a perfectly logical explanation.
It may even have suggested the cowboy characters for
his later novel, *Lord Malquist and Mr Moon*.

But the most important achievement of his five
months in Berlin was the writing of a one-act verse
burlesque called *Rosencrantz and Guildenstern Meet*

King Lear. All of the plays written by the grantees in
Berlin were given studio productions by amateur actors. Stoppard thought that his effort was unspeakably
bad, but Saunders urged him to expand it into a full-
length play. On his return to England in October 1964,
Stoppard scrapped the original and began again with its
subject.

The full-length *Rosencrantz and Guildenstern Are
Dead* that eventually launched Stoppard's career as a
playwright bears little resemblance to the earlier work,
for the full-length play ends where the short one began.
Stoppard thus describes the creative process that led
from one to the other: "If you write a play about Rosencrantz and Guildenstern in England, you can't count on
people knowing who they are and how they got there.
So one tended to get back into the end of *Hamlet* a bit.
But the explanations were always partial and ambiguous, so one went back a bit further into the plot, and as
soon as I started doing this I totally lost interest in
England. The interesting thing was them at
Elsinore."[18]

Although *Rosencrantz and Guildenstern Are Dead*
was completed in the spring of 1965, two more years
were to pass before it became a London success. In his
article "The Definite Maybe" (*Author*, Spring 1967),
Stoppard chronicled the progress of the play under op-
tions taken by different companies. Meanwhile, he
supported himself and Jose Ingle, whom he married in
1965, by writing episodes for a BBC Radio serial about
an Arab medical student in London. These were translated into Arabic and broadcast on the Overseas Service. According to Ewing, "he alternated with another
author, and every other week he was paid forty pounds
for five episodes. As far as I know, he had never met an
Arab in his life. But the job kept him going for about
nine months."[19]

Ewing was also amused to notice that the
financially troubled writer would go by taxi rather than

by subway or bus to request advances on his salary, "as if he knew that his time would come."[20] Stoppard simply explains that he has "always treated money as the stuff with which you purchase time."[21] His comment on the Arab serial, that "as a piece of writing it did not exist,"[22] has proved true in actuality as well as metaphorically: the BBC claims to have kept no copy of these scripts.

Despite the impressive volume of his published work, writing does not come easily to Stoppard. In 1965, he was contracted to write a novel, which he "finally started two days before it was due. I worked out that if I wrote 30,000 words a day, I could still get it done in time."[23] He said in an interview with Kathleen Halton (*Vogue*, October 15, 1967) that, even in his newspaper days, his "Kamikaze pilot mentality" prevented him from starting until it was almost too late, and that the copyboy would then have to carry his weekly columns sentence by sentence to the newsroom in order to meet the deadline. Overcoming that block is for him the major effort in the process of writing:

I half commit myself to some distant future date. I often talk to someone about it and suggest that in six months it will be done, so I set up a kind of deadline. But most of the intervening period disappears in a kind of anxious state of walking about. You cannot start until you know what you want to do, and you do not know what you want to do until you start. That is catch-22. Panic breaks that circle. Finally a certain force in the accumulated material begins to form a pattern.[24]

Stoppard's only novel, *Lord Malquist and Mr Moon*, was published in England in 1966, at about the same time that *Rosencrantz and Guildenstern Are Dead* was first staged. When the play's then current option ran out, permission was granted to the amateur Oxford Theatre Group to present it on the Fringe of the Edinburgh Festival in August. According to an actress in that original production (Janet Watts, *The Guardian*,

May 21, 1973), the production was in trouble when Stoppard arrived in Edinburgh for the last few rehearsals. Not only had the director quit; the actors were anxious about the play, which seemed too repetitive. The situation did not faze Stoppard, since all his hopes were pinned on the novel. He jokingly explained the repetitions as "a massive typing error," raised the morale of the troupe, and brought some order to the direction.

Stoppard stayed for the first two or three performances and felt that the play was received "politely rather than with hilarity,"[25] confirming his belief that it would be the novel that made his reputation rather than the play. On the train back to London, however, while scanning the pages of the *Observer* for a notice on *Lord Malquist and Mr Moon,* he came across the play review that created a turning point in his career. Ronald Bryden called *Rosencrantz and Guildenstern Are Dead* "the most brilliant debut by a young playwright since John Arden." The novel, by contrast, sold fewer than seven hundred copies in its first printing.

As dramaturg for the National Theatre under Sir Laurence Olivier, Kenneth Tynan was always looking for stageworthy new scripts. He wrote in his *New Yorker* "Profile" on Stoppard (December 17, 1977): "Minutes after reading Bryden's piece, I cabled Stoppard requesting a script. Olivier liked it as much as I did, and within a week we had bought it." Stoppard attended rehearsals, making minor cuts and revisions in the script and, at Olivier's suggestion, adding one entirely new scene. At twenty-nine, Stoppard became the youngest playwright ever to have his work performed by the National Theatre. The production brought rave reviews, as well as the major dramatic prizes of the year.

Stoppard then spent three and a half months in the United States, helping with rehearsals for the New

York production of *Rosencrantz and Guildenstern Are Dead*, which opened seven months after the one in London. Again the critical response was one of overwhelming praise. *Rosencrantz and Guildenstern Are Dead* won both the Antoinette Perry (Tony) Award and the Drama Critics' Circle Award for Best Play of 1967–1968.

The wry observations occasioned by Stoppard's first visit to America were characteristic of his preoccupation with language, and with the distortions of logic that it can perpetrate. Amused at Americans' everyday exposure to hyperbole, he mentioned to Dan Sullivan, in a *New York Times* interview (August 29, 1967), the fact that one cannot find a "small" egg in the United States, only "mediums, larges, extra-larges, and jumbos." When a television announcer said "stand by for an important message," Stoppard recalls that, "like a cluck, I stood by." The moral to be drawn from all of this is, he commented, that "devaluation of the language is more serious than devaluation of the pound."

In 1968 Stoppard was in London in March for the opening of *Enter A Free Man* (a revised version of *A Walk on the Water,*) in New York in May for the first American publication of *Lord Malquist and Mr Moon*, and back in London in June for the opening of his one-act mystery spoof, *The Real Inspector Hound*. At the same time, however, he found himself writing less and less. The summer of 1968 was the beginning of what he called "a very unprolific period" that lasted two years.[26]

After the success of *Rosencrantz and Guildenstern Are Dead*, Stoppard felt that for the first time in seven or eight years he was no longer under pressure, albeit self-imposed, to achieve recognition. He needed a little time to enjoy the feeling of success, which turned out to be less thrilling than he had imagined it. There was, too, the fear that his next full-length play might not live up to everyone's expectations. The one-act plays, *After Magritte* and *Dogg's Our Pet*, and several radio and television plays were all that kept his name before the public until the opening of *Jumpers* early in 1972.

Jumpers took two years to write, because, after deciding "to write a play about an ethical question in terms of academics," Stoppard set up for himself an intensive reading program in philosophy. He told interviewer Barry Norman (*The Times*, November 11, 1972) that he had wanted "to make sure that what I thought were my penetrating insights weren't simply the average conclusions of a first-year philosophy student, which they invariably turned out to be." Derek Marlowe has said of Stoppard's working method: "For Tom, writing a play is like sitting for an examination. He spends ages on research, does all the necessary cramming, reads all the relevant books, and then gestates the results. Once he's passed the exam—with the public and the critics—he forgets all about it and moves on to the next subject."[27]

Stoppard has claimed that he cannot invent plots, but that he was trying to kick the habit of hanging his plays on other people's plots (*Rosencrantz and Guildenstern Are Dead* on Shakespeare's *Hamlet*, *Travesties* on Oscar Wilde's *The Importance of Being Earnest*, *The Real Inspector Hound* on Agatha Christie's *The Mousetrap*, for example). One of his solutions is to posit a series of "ambushes"—large ones, such as a body falling out of a cupboard, or microscopic ones, like an unexpected word in a sentence. He may be joking at his own expense when he has Rosencrantz say in Act 3: "Incidents! All we get is incidents! Dear God, is it too much to expect a little sustained action?!"

The slow rate at which Stoppard writes is a function of two major preoccupations: his desire to construct an action with an underlying logic that is absolutely unshakable, and a mania for injecting interest and color into every individual line as a precaution, lest the dramatic situation itself not hold the audience's attention. He illustrated the latter concern, in a lecture at the University of California at Santa Barbara in 1977, by reading from the various working drafts of *Travesties*. In the earliest version, he had Tristan Tzara address James Joyce as "you blarney-arsed bog-eating Irish pig," but in the final version the line had become: "By God, you suspicious streak of Irish puke!" And he explained that "all this takes *weeks*."[28]

The two years between the beginning of his research on *Jumpers* in 1970 and its production in 1972 was also the period of dissolution of Stoppard's first marriage. Jose Ingle and Stoppard had met when they both lived in the same low-rent apartment building. They supported each other's career ambitions during several lean years, but his sudden success caused an imbalance that the marriage could not survive. They separated in 1970 and were divorced in 1972. He won custody of their two sons, Oliver and Barnaby.

Married again in 1972 to Dr. Miriam Moore-Robinson, Stoppard now has two more sons, William and Edmund. His wife has her own successful career as the medical director of Syntex Pharmaceuticals, a company that specializes in birth-control research. She also became a well-known BBC Television personality, as a panelist on the quiz show *Call My Bluff*. Her vivacious fielding of popular science questions—on biology, zoology, sex—has earned her greater celebrity with the British television audience than her husband. They live modestly in a book-filled house on three acres in Iver Heath, a suburb of London. Stoppard prefers being at home with his family to anything else. His insistence upon his need for domestic stability in order to write has been corroborated by the increased volume, variety, and quality of his writing since 1972.

The first draft of *Jumpers* was nearly finished late in the summer of 1971, when the National Theatre's play-selection deadline for the following season made an immediate reading imperative, if it was to be considered. With no time to get the play typed, Stoppard asked if he might read it himself to the selection committee. He met with Sir Laurence Olivier, Kenneth Tynan, John Dexter, and Michael Blakemore at Tynan's house one afternoon. Olivier had come directly from a very demanding rehearsal and became drowsy after a few glasses of wine. Stoppard had written his characters' names on individual cards, which he held up while reading, to indicate who was speaking. Before long the cards were totally jumbled, and the play was incomprehensible to the listeners. Tynan's *New Yorker* "Profile" (December 19, 1977) gives his recollection of Stoppard, "desperate in the gathering dusk, frantically shuffling his precious pages and brandishing his cards, like a panicky magician whose tricks are blowing up in his face." After two hours of this, Stoppard left, feeling stunned and miserable. He was unable to continue working on the play, until he received a reassuring letter from Dexter encouraging him to finish it.

Jumpers opened at the Old Vic on February 2, 1972, and consolidated Stoppard's reputation. With his second full-length play successfully produced by the National Theatre, he was no longer a one-shot celebrity riding on beginner's luck. *Jumpers* is, in fact, the play in which Stoppard makes his best use of the resources of the stage; it is, to date, his masterpiece.

In his article "Yes, We Have No Bananas" (*The Guardian*, December 10, 1971), Stoppard gives his amusing account of being distracted from rehearsals of *Jumpers* at the "Established Theatre," by the irresistible fun of writing for and working with Ed Berman in an "Alternative Theatre" situation. Since Stoppard had a month between the completion of his final draft of *Jumpers* and its first rehearsal, Berman cajoled him into writing a play for one of his four Inter-Action theater groups.

It was Berman who had first produced *After Ma-gritte,* in a twelve-by-twelve-foot space at the Green Banana Restaurant in April 1970. Now Berman wanted a play for The Dogg's Troupe, previously known as Professor R.L. Dogg's Human Flea Circus. (Berman used the pen name R.L. Dogg for his poetry, in order that eventual library card-catalogue listings would stand testament to its true worth: Dogg, R.L.—"doggerel.") Stoppard wrote *Dogg's Our Pet* for The Dogg's Troupe. It was performed in December 1971, at the Almost Free Theatre.

Berman and Stoppard have each expressed admiration for the other's work. Stoppard's *Guardian* article describes Berman's dynamic efforts in the area of community arts (theatre in the streets, schools, mental homes, and other public institutions): "Berman makes it happen, raises money, works one hundred hours a week, writes, directs, sings, acts, sweeps the floor, and negotiates for more money." Berman simply declares Stoppard to be a genius.

Four years after *Dogg's Our Pet,* Berman again requested a play from Stoppard—specifically a play about America, for a lunch-hour Bicentennial series at the Almost Free Theatre. The American-born Berman wanted the play to commemorate his naturalization as a British citizen. Faced by a deadline and unable to do anything with the given premise, Stoppard finally threw out all his false starts and worked instead on another idea he had been keeping in mind for future use. This became *Dirty Linen,* a farce on the subject of sex scandals in Parliament. Stoppard acknowledges his debt to a God who "looks after English playwrights" for inspiring the idea that he need only have his parliamentary committee adjourn for fifteen minutes in the course of *Dirty Linen* in order to interpolate the play Berman had requested. The stage setting could be used for a brief sketch in which two civil servants consider an

American's application for naturalization as a British subject. To the critics, Stoppard's little joke, inserted as a favor to a friend and given its own title, *New-Found-Land*, was another triumph of inventiveness: the intermission-filler makes a sort of dramatic sandwich of the evening of theater.

In 1979 Berman founded a new troupe called British American Repertory Company—the acronym BARC being most appropriate for an organization headed by Professor Dogg. In an earlier attempt to tour some Inter-Action productions to the United States, Berman had been blocked by the protectionist policies of British and American Actors' Equity associations, both of which allow only stars to perform in the other country. A British play imported to New York, for example, must be recast with American actors.

Berman took a big step toward his goal of reunifying the English-speaking theater when BARC became the first company ever to be jointly recognized by both British and American Actors' Equity associations. He achieved this by forming a company composed of an equal number of actors and stage managers from each country, with plans to tour for five months a year in each country. Berman auditioned about 900 actors in New York and in London to select his company of twelve, and he claims that, unless one reads the program notes, an audience member cannot tell which are American and which are British. BARC's premiere production was *Dogg's Hamlet, Cahoot's Macbeth*, written especially for that occasion by Tom Stoppard.

Stoppard's work has continued to be varied and unpredictable. He told Janet Watts (*The Guardian*, March 21, 1973): "I would like ultimately before being carried out feet first to have done a bit of absolutely everything. Really without any evidence for any talent in those directions, I find it very hard to turn down offers to write an underwater ballet for dolphins or a play for a motorcyclist on the wall of death." It was that willingness to take risks in tackling the untried that led Stoppard to write an English version of Federico García Lorca's *House of Bernarda Alba* (even though he knows no Spanish), to direct a production of Garson Kanin's *Born Yesterday* for the Greenwich Theatre, to write three screenplays, and to edit *Hamlet* down to fifteen minutes for Ed Berman's Inter-Action. Perhaps most astonishingly, he met André Previn's challenge to write a play that would incorporate an entire symphony orchestra in the action (even though he claimed to know little about music); *Every Good Boy Deserves Favour* is a theatrical tour de force in which innovative theatrical techniques animate the ideas and the entertainment values.

As the number of Stoppard's successful full-length plays multiplied, he was frequently confronted with questions about his apparent lack of interest in writing socially conscious, or political, plays. Of course, Stoppard had always written plays of ideas disguised as comedy, or as he says, plays that "make serious points by flinging a custard pie around the stage for a couple of hours."[29] He has also said: "I write plays because writing dialogue is the only respectable way of contradicting yourself. I'm the kind of person who embarks on an endless leapfrog down the great moral issues. I put a position, rebut it, refute the rebuttal, and rebut the refutation." At an early point in his thinking about the play that was to become *Travesties*, for example, he conceived of it as "a two-act thing, with one act a Dadaist play on Communist ideology and the other an ideological functional drama about Dadaists."[30] Ultimately and perhaps partially in response to those looking for political content, Stoppard used *Travesties* to examine the question of whether an artist has any obligation at all to justify himself in political terms.

During most of his career to the time of this writing, Stoppard has resisted the urge to cheapen or exploit the art of the theater simply in order to propound a particular point of view. However, two observations must be made with regard to this attitude. One is that he does have serious convictions about political, social, and moral issues. His political views tend to be conservative, and they are inseparable from moral judgments. His fellow playwright James Saunders has surmised that Stoppard hesitates to express opinions because he still thinks of himself as a guest in Britain, in which case any criticism would be impolite.[31] In 1974 Stoppard commented somewhat facetiously on his own work: "I think that in future I must stop compromising my plays with this whiff of social application. They must be entirely untouched by any suspicion of usefulness. I should have the courage of my lack of convictions."

The second point to be made about the nonpolitical nature of Stoppard's theater is that it may be changing. There is some indication that his work is moving toward a more direct confrontation with issues like human rights in totalitarian countries. In February 1977, as a member of the Committee Against Psychiatric Abuse, traveling with the Assistant Director of the British section of Amnesty International, he visited several persecuted Soviet dissidents in Moscow and Leningrad, and subsequently reported his observations in *The Sunday Times* (February 27, 1977). In June, he traveled to Czechoslovakia to meet playwright Václav Havel, who had been released on May 20 after a four-month imprisonment by the Czech government for his nonconformism. Stoppard must have been profoundly shaken by his return visit to the country of his birth, especially in the light of his statement to Kenneth Tynan: "Of all the systems that are on offer, the one I don't want is the one that denies freedom of expression—no matter what its allegedly redeeming virtues may be."[32] His next two major works were the play-with-orchestra, *Every Good Boy Deserves Favour*, which is set in an asylum for "antisocial malcontents," and the television drama, *Professional Foul*, which concerns freedom of speech in Czechoslovakia.

Stoppard now sees that the immorality inherent in a totalitarian society that restricts individual rights and inflicts violence upon nonconformists is a broad, timeless issue that merits his artistic consideration. He would be wasting his talent to write about the exceptional instance of violence inflicted upon the underprivileged in a free society like England, as leftist spokesmen have called for him to do. In a sense, however, he has finally responded to those pressures, in that his 1978 drama, *Night and Day*, takes up the problem of moral responsibilities and practical failings of a free press. According to Sheridan Morley (*Playbill*, New York, June 1979), "his play, in its Shavian-debate structure, is generally regarded to be the first time in the theater that he has climbed down off the Scrabble board of his own remarkable linguistic talents and tackled a tangible issue." It remains to be seen whether this new effort will prove compatible with Stoppard's artistry.

Another change for Stoppard may be an unprecedented willingness to explore his characters' emotions. He had always consciously and conscientiously avoided putting himself or his intimately personal preoccupations into his work. Early in his career as a playwright, he told Giles Cooper (*Transatlantic Review*, Summer 1968): "I am sensitive about self-revelation. I distrust it. I've written very little which could be said to be even remotely autobiographical and I've been subsequently somewhat embarrassed by what I have written." Yet he has always understood that any work of art, beginning with the choice of subject matter, will unavoidably reveal something about the artist. He went on to say, for example, that Rosencrantz and Guildenstern "both add up to me in many ways in the sense that they're carrying out a dialogue which I carry out with myself. One of them is fairly intellectual, fairly incisive; the other is thicker, nicer in a curious way, more sympathetic. There's a leader and the led. Retrospectively, with all benefit of other people's comments and enthusiasms and so on, it just seems a classic case of self-revelation even though it isn't about this fellow who wrote his first novel."

Stoppard describes himself, like his plays, as "seriousness compromised by frivolity." With *Night and Day*, at last, the frivolity is downplayed by a sincere and not wholly unsuccessful effort to create real people with genuine emotions. *Night and Day* actually begins with one of Stoppard's own early fantasies about journalism—that of the reporter being pinned down by hostile shelling in the course of his dutifully zealous pursuit of good copy for the readers back home.

Having been a major playwright for only a dozen years, Stoppard is still relatively young. It will be interesting to see whether or not he continues to fear that any personal or "soft" element allowed into his work will cause it to "get rotten like fruit." In metaphorical opposition to plays that decompose like fruit are plays that are solid like ashtrays: "You make an ashtray and come back next year and it's still the same ashtray. Beckett and Pinter have a lot more chance of writing ashtrays because they've thrown out all the potential soft stuff."[33] In any case, Stoppard will probably continue to surprise those who follow his career. It is part of his credo. He told Mel Gussow: "I don't respect people who are rigorously consistent. That denotes a kind of atrophy of spirit. I like people who repudiate everything they've written every five years. Probably up until the age of fifty that's a healthy thing to do."[34]

2

Home Free:
Rosencrantz and Guildenstern Are Dead

With the success of *Rosencrantz and Guildenstern Are Dead,* Tom Stoppard—to use the vocabulary of gamesmanship that is so important to his plays—was "home free." He had won acceptance in a language and a culture in which he had previously considered himself a guest. He had played by the rules and made the first team: to all the world, Tom Stoppard was a British playwright. Although some of his subsequent plays have surpassed its artistry, *Rosencrantz and Guildenstern Are Dead* is still the work most widely identified with Stoppard's name.

The most obvious sign of a major new playwriting talent at work was its brashness and ingenuity in dramatizing the flip side of *Hamlet.* It seemed a stroke of genius to make "heroes" of two of Shakespeare's most nondescript characters, barely distinguishable one from the other, while the complex intrigues of the court of Elsinore became a vague peripheral activity occurring in other rooms of the palace.

Although the British theatre was still reasonably vigorous after a decade of "kitchen dramas" by "angry young men" (in what Harold Clurman called "an ever increasing overall atmosphere of grubbiness and decay which has marked English dramaturgy since 1956"[1]), Stoppard's play brought a blast of fresh air onto the scene by lifting out of the familiar working-class setting into the pictorially bleak realm of ideas. In this respect, it must be noted that Samuel Beckett's *Waiting for Godot* is as important a context for Stoppard's play as is Shakespeare's *Hamlet*. This influence, as well as the play's kinship with Pirandello's *Six Characters in Search of an Author*, will be examined after a summary analysis of what happens on stage in *Rosencrantz and Guildenstern Are Dead*.

The play opens with a game underway. It is the first of a number of games played by Rosencrantz and Guildenstern to pass the time while they wait for some meaningful assigned task, or at least for some explanation of why they have been summoned to Elsinore. It will not take the spectator long to decide that they exemplify twentieth-century man's groping for a sense of identity and purpose in modern life. Guildenstern has been spinning coins for Rosencrantz to call, and Rosencrantz has correctly called "heads" over seventy-five times before any actual dialogue begins. Of the two, only Guildenstern is astonished at this inexplicable breakdown of the laws of probability.

To insure that the audience enters the world of the play on the abstract level of an intellectual exercise, Stoppard sidesteps the ground rules of traditional dramaturgy. For examply, Rosencrantz and Guildenstern do not use each other's names until over ten minutes into the play, when they must introduce themselves to the Player and his troupe, and even then they confuse the issue, allowing only the alertest of spectators to figure out which is which. Nor is there any indication of place until Rosencrantz says, just before the Player's entrance, "That's why we're here. (*He looks around, seems doubtful, then the explanation.*) Travelling." And we understand at last that they are on the road to Elsinore.

Rosencrantz and Guildenstern are, in Stoppard's mind, two sides of one temperament. Although they

cannot themselves keep their identities straight, the
audience gradually perceives that one of them (Guildenstern) is more cerebral than the other, has greater
awareness of the ambiguity of their situation, and
struggles with it. Rosencrantz, the more passive one,
operates on instinct; he has no capacity for astonish-
ment; the few times that he initiates a topic for discussion, the topic is death. The exposition—indeed, the
entire play—reveals only one piece of information
about their past: that a messenger had awakened them
before dawn with a royal summons, "a matter of extreme urgency" and "no questions asked." A few interpolated lines from *Hamlet* later remind us that Rosencrantz and Guildenstern were school chums of the
melancholy prince, but beyond these scraps of characterization Stoppard chooses to give the heroes of his
play no more substance than Shakespeare allotted them
as walk-ons.

A troupe of itinerant actors is overjoyed to meet
Rosencrantz and Guildenstern on the road, for they
represent a potential audience. The troupe's spokesman, the Player, tries to interest them in a performance. Times being what they are, he is even willing to
profane the tragedian's art by purveying instead a por-
nographic exhibition in which, for a few guilders more,
the two spectators may participate. The Player's offer to
"do on stage the things that are supposed to happen off"
not only carries sexual innuendo, but is a statement of
Stoppard's technique in his play's relation to *Hamlet*.

Instead of booking a performance, Guildenstern
engages the Player in betting on the tosses of the coin.
"Heads" wins repeatedly, as Guildenstern knew from
experience that it would. Temporarily without money,
the tragedians offer in payment the boy player Alfred in
a skirt. He is the innocent victim with nothing left to
lose. Guildenstern breaks the fourth-wall convention of
the stage when he says, "You and I, Alfred—we could
create a dramatic precedent here," meaning that they

could commit a homosexual act in front of the live theater audience. Stoppard may have been chiding authors of the scatological plays and performance groups like the Living Theater that were so prevalent in the mid-1960s, by having Guildenstern tell Alfred that "this is no way to fill the theatres of Europe."

Guildenstern asks for a play to pay off the bet, and the tragedians prepare to comply. Meanwhile, Rosencrantz picks up the coin that was left lying on the ground. His discovery that this one is "tails" pulls the rug out from under our now-established belief in an absurd universe where laws of probability do not operate.

A sudden change in the lighting suggests a cinematic jump in time and space. Rosencrantz and Guildenstern have not moved, but they witness, instead of the tragedians' performance, a wordless encounter between Ophelia and Hamlet, just like the one Ophelia describes to Polonius in Act 2, scene 1 of *Hamlet*. The first fifty lines of Act 2, scene 2 are incorporated, uncut, from Shakespeare, except that Stoppard has his protagonists move to a spot downstage instead of making an exit. In this scene, Claudius and Gertrude ask them to draw Hamlet "on to pleasures" and to "glean what afflicts him." Stoppard superimposes a visual joke on Shakespeare's text, by having Rosencrantz and Guildenstern bob up and down in badly timed, clownlike bows, while Claudius says, "Thanks Rosencrantz and gentle Guildenstern" and Gertrude tries to correct the identification with "Thanks Guildenstern and gentle Rosencrantz."

After their audience with the King and Queen, Rosencrantz and Guildenstern realize that they are caught up in a sequence of events that they are powerless to understand, much less to alter so as to control their own destinies. They are frightened, but there is a kind of comfort, too, in having one's choices determined in advance, in this case by the structure of Shakespeare's play. They fall back upon their habit of playing games—simple wordplay at first, then a complex match of serving and returning questions with tennislike rules and vocabulary. When Hamlet crosses the back of the stage, absorbed in a book, they are reminded of their purpose at court and tackle a game of role-playing. Guildenstern pretends to be Hamlet, and Rosencrantz practices asking questions that might enable them to "glean what afflicts him"—a game at which they are quite inept. The act ends with Hamlet returning to greet his two boyhood friends.

Act 2 of Stoppard's play begins near the end of Rosencrantz and Guildenstern's longest scene in Shakespeare's play, their first interview with Hamlet. Stoppard bridges that scene with an intermission, but summarizes it afterward in a deliberately banal, statistical fashion, when his duo discuss what they have gleaned. Hamlet actually did ask twenty-seven questions and answer only three in Shakespeare's text. The substance of what he has revealed to them, without the style, is flatly recalled by Rosencrantz: "Denmark's a prison and he'd rather live in a nutshell; some shadow-play about the nature of ambition, which never got down to cases, and finally one direct question which might have led somewhere and led in fact to his illuminating claim to tell a hack from a handsaw."

They argue pointlessly over the time of day and over compass directions, their confusion in these matters mirroring their ontological disorientation. Another game is initiated when Rosencrantz invites Guildenstern to choose in which fist he has hidden a coin. After three wrong guesses, Guildenstern sees that Rosencrantz has cheated: both fists are empty. But the joke backfires on Rosencrantz, for he cannot find his coin. His puzzled search for it becomes a running gag throughout the rest of the act. One might see the lost coin as an objective correlative of their ability to determine a course of action—a choice that seemed foreordained but is now even more frighteningly out of their hands. The tragedians, newly arrived at the castle, reproach Rosencrantz and Guildenstern for having slipped away in the middle of their performance on the road. This confrontation affords Stoppard another opportunity for some discourse upon his favorite subject: the nature of art. The point is made, in a wry teasing fashion, that the actor, or any artist, exposes himself mercilessly, that he bares his ego and his very soul as an offering to his audience. But, if the audience chooses to ignore the work, then the artist's sacrifice becomes a meaningless, and even obscene, act.

Rosencrantz and Guildenstern try to take credit for arranging the tragedians' performance at court, but the Player one-ups their every claim, until Guildenstern breaks down and confesses their insecurity. The Player gently offers them a philosophy of life, which would seem to be the antithesis of the artist's own search for meaning, but which serves the needs of the little man in coping with forces beyond his comprehension. He tells them not to question the way things are, but to proceed by accepting appearance for truth. This leads to a discussion of Hamlet's condition and a brief, strikingly rhythmic alliterative sequence that sums up centuries of scholarly debate over the question of whether Hamlet is really mad:

> GUIL: He's—melancholy.
> PLAYER: Melancholy?
> ROS: Mad.
> PLAYER: How is he mad?
> ROS: Ah. (*To* GUIL:) How is he mad?
> GUIL: More morose than mad, perhaps.
> PLAYER: Melancholy.
> GUIL: Moody.
> ROS: He has moods.

PLAYER: Of moroseness?
GUIL: Madness. And yet.
ROS: Quite.
GUIL: For instance.
ROS: He talks to himself, which might be madness.
GUIL: If he didn't talk sense, which he does.
ROS: Which suggests the opposite.
PLAYER: Of what?

Small pause.

GUIL: I think I have it. A man talking sense to himself is no madder than a man talking nonsense not to himself.
ROS: Or just as mad.
GUIL: Or just as mad.
ROS: And he does both.
GUIL: So there you are.
ROS: Stark raving sane.

When the Player leaves them, Rosencrantz and Guildenstern must face their boredom again. Rosencrantz initiates a conversation about death and talks himself around to the conclusion that "life in a box is better than no life at all," a metaphor for the play by Shakespeare, which boxes them in, despite Stoppard's having given them a new life. Claudius and Gertrude sweep onto the scene, exchange thirty lines of dialogue from Act 3, scene 1 of *Hamlet*, and exit again. A moment later, Hamlet enters, apparently lost in thought. The two lines of his that we are able to hear when he exits in pursuit of Ophelia indicate, to those in the audience who know Shakespeare's *Hamlet*, that he has just been brooding about whether "to be or not to be."

The mood switches abruptly when the Queen reenters and Rosencrantz impetuously and uncharacteristically puts his hand over her eyes and says "Guess who?!" But it turns out to be Alfred, in a wig and costume identical to the Queen's. The sight gag of mistaken identity serves two dramatic functions besides its humorous one: it reinforces the theme of blurred

boundaries between art and life, and it plants the notion of the interchangeability of the tragedians and the
court royalty, upon which the final tableau of the play
will depend.

The tragedians rehearse the dumbshow they are to
perform for the court, but they are interrupted by the
return of Hamlet and Ophelia, who are finishing their
scene together. Hamlet exits, after telling her to go to a
nunnery. Ophelia, upstage, presumably gives her
speech, "O what a noble mind is here o'erthrown!"
However, it is inaudible to Stoppard's audience, since
he keeps the tragedians before us, downstage, perhaps
embarrassed at having witnessed the encounter.

The sequence lasting from the exit of the royalty
until the blackout three-quarters of the way through
the act—a long passage in which the Player discusses
the tragedians' art with Rosencrantz and Guildenstern
and narrates the action of the play that will be performed for the court—is the emblem of Stoppard's
larger play. That is, this sequence is a miniaturized
reflection of the entire play, and it illuminates the
meaning of the play.[2] The Player tells the two that
"events must play themselves out to aesthetic, moral,
and logical conclusion." This is truly a statement of
Stoppard's own preoccupations as a playwright; it will
be seen that he scrupulously satisfies all three re-
quirements, in this, and in each of his other plays.

The specific artistic design in the tragedians' own
work is, the Player says, to reach "the point where
everyone who is marked for death dies." The tragedians then mime the action in *Hamlet* while the Player
narrates. The story they rehearse goes much further
than the play-within-the-play that one sees in *Hamlet*.
They include the melancholy prince's closet scene with
his mother the queen, his stabbing of the old chief
councillor behind the arras, and his being sent to England with "two smiling accomplices—friends—cour-

tiers—two spies," who bear a letter that seals their deaths.

Thus are Rosencrantz and Guildenstern fore-warned of their own deaths, even to the extent that the two spies executed in the mime show wear costumes identical to theirs. And yet Rosencrantz and Guilden-stern refuse to see themselves in the story, despite Guildenstern's expressed desire for "art to mirror life." Guildenstern reacts to the mimed execution sequence by insisting that death is one thing that cannot be acted:

No, no, no . . . you've got it all wrong . . . you can't act death. The *fact* of it is nothing to do with seeing it happen—it's not gasps and blood and falling about—that isn't what makes it death. It's just a man failing to reappear, that's all—now you see him, now you don't, that's the only thing that's real: here one minute and gone the next and never coming back—an exit, unobtrusive and unannounced, a disappearance gather-ing weight as it goes on, until, finally, it is heavy with death.

There is a sudden blackout, during which are heard lines from the end of the players' scene in *Hamlet:* "Give o'er the play!" "Lights, lights, lights!" When the lights come up, Rosencrantz and Guilden-stern are again alone together, lying on the ground in the positions previously occupied by the two actor-spies. At this point in *Hamlet*—that is, immediately following the disruption of the players' performance be-fore the court—Shakespeare gave Rosencrantz and Guildenstern a second interview with Hamlet. This is the one in which they are compared to recorders: "Though you can fret me, yet you cannot play upon me." In explaining why he chose to omit this scene and any reference to it in his play, Stoppard has referred to the Grove Press "Discussion Guide" for his play, which suggests that the student reread the scenes in *Hamlet* in which Rosencrantz and Guildenstern appear, and then explain why Stoppard uses the "sponge" scene but not the "recorders" scene.[3] Dismissing the tendency of literary criticism toward overintellectualized interpretation of the subject, which has nothing to do with the experience of watching a performance, Stoppard declared, "The correct answer is, because we are not sitting in a classroom, we are sitting in a theatre, and we have been sitting there for rather a long time."[4]

The blackout marks a kind of cinematic jump in time, because the next interpolated lines from Shakespeare are Claudius's request to Rosencrantz and Guildenstern, in Act 4, scene 1, that they find out from Hamlet where he hid Polonius's body. This speech and their subsequent talk with Hamlet (4.2), also omitted in the original version, were added at Sir Laurence Olivier's suggestion, because it was "the one time in the play when they were given an actual specific duty to fulfill."[5] The action that follows from Claudius's directive is a selection of moments from *Hamlet*, intertwined with sight gags built upon Rosencrantz and Guildenstern's insecurity and incomprehension. They are like vaudeville clowns trying to pass themselves off as worthy of appearing in a tragedy.

A change of lighting signals another leap in time and space that is eventually pinpointed in Rosencrantz and Guildenstern's dialogue. On Claudius's orders, they are now taking Hamlet to England, but they must still rely upon each other for companionship. They are left to their own devices while Hamlet converses with a soldier from Fortinbras's army (4.4) and wanders off for a soliloquy. Within the overall structure of the play, this segment is too long and anticlimactic. We do not at this point need to be reminded of Rosencrantz and Guildenstern's confusion and aimlessness. The sequence serves only as a transition between the palace and the boat to England. Act 2 ends for the two flunkies on a note of false hope and metaphysical disorientation.

The boat in Act 3, like the play-within-the-play in act 2, is a self-contained and delimited preserve iso-

lated from the surrounding chaos. Guildenstern sees
the boat as a "safe area in the game of tag," because the
question of choosing one's own direction does not even
arise; here one is "free."

When their conversation bogs down, Rosencrantz
and Guildenstern resort to their game of choosing
which fist holds the coin, and now Guildenstern wins
six times in a row. He discovers that Rosencrantz, hoping to make him happy, had money in both hands.
Rosencrantz's cheating may be seen as a way of taking
destiny into his own hands and controlling the laws of
probability, whether the universe in which those laws
operate is absurd or conventional. It is Rosencrantz and
Guildenstern's tragic flaw that they are unable to do
this outside the structured framework of a game.

They discuss the possible nature of their diplomatic mission to England. They get caught up in a role-
playing game, Rosencrantz taking the part of the King
of England and Guildenstern speaking for the two of
them. In their earnestness, they tear open the letter
they are carrying from Claudius to the King of England.
They learn that they are the bearers of an order for
Hamlet's execution. Rosencrantz's response is an emotional one: Hamlet is their friend. Guildenstern offers a
list of reasons—rationalizations—for not interfering
"with the designs of fate or even of Kings." They tie up
the letter again and go to sleep.

By moonlight Hamlet goes to the sleeping pair,
purloins the letter, and replaces it with another. In the
morning the sound of a recorder announces to Rosencrantz and Guildenstern that the tragedians are present
on the boat. Having offended the king with their performance at court, they had to make a fast getaway in
costume, and are traveling as stowaways. Discussing
their situation with the Player, Guildenstern says:

We have, for the while, secured, or blundered into, our re-
lease, for the while. Spontaneity and whim are the order of

the day. Other wheels are turning but they are not our concern. We can breathe. We can relax. We can do what we like and say what we like to whomever we like, without restriction.

But Rosencrantz qualifies the last statement: "Within limits, of course." The literal meaning of these words—that the boat trip affords some respite from their functioning as mere pawns—is echoed in another sense: that, just now, they are free from the confinement of Shakespeare's plot, since it contains no scene set on the boat. There is a subconscious awareness, however, that they are among the "loose ends" that will have to be tied up in the denouement of *Hamlet*.

It is significant that, immediately following this speech, Hamlet is momentarily freed from the confines of his role as a princely tragic hero and given a bit of comic business. He comes down to the footlights which represent the side of the boat, clears his throat and spits into the audience. A split second later come the consequences of spitting into the wind: he claps his hand to his eye and wipes his face.

A pirate attack brings shouting, pratfalls, and general commotion. Hamlet, the Player, Rosencrantz and Guildenstern jump into the three large barrels on deck, where they remain until the sound of fighting dies away in the dark. When the lights come up and the barrel lids are cautiously raised, Hamlet is missing. (We recall from Shakespeare's text that the pirates saved his life and took him back to Denmark.) Rosencrantz says, "He's dead as far as we're concerned," and the Player responds with a closer truth: "Or we are as far as he is."

Without Hamlet, Rosencrantz and Guildenstern feel more adrift and purposeless than ever. They reopen the letter to confirm that they did indeed have a mission to accomplish, and they read an order for their own execution. Guildenstern agonizes: "Who are we that so much should converge on our little deaths?" The crowning blow is that they are "still, finally, to be denied an explanation."

"In our experience, most things end in death," says the Player. This is scant consolation, since the tragedians' "experience" is not life but a mere representation of it. Guildenstern is angered to the point of snatching the Player's dagger and—as if to teach him the real meaning of death, for which "there is no applause"—drives it into his throat. The Player clutches at the wound, staggers, falls, and, while Guildenstern watches and becomes hysterical, dies, A moment later, he gets to his feet and receives the congratulations of his troupe: his death was totally believable to anyone unaware that the prop dagger had a retractable blade. This death, therefore, was as real as actual death. Since Rosencrantz and Guildenstern were completely taken in by it, the Player has finally demonstrated irrefutably what he had tried to explain all along: that art has greater reality than life.

It might be argued that it is this understanding that enables Rosencrantz and Guildenstern to go to their deaths. In *Hamlet,* we assume that Rosencrantz and Guildenstern meet their fates blindly, ignorant of the contents of the letter they carry to the English king. But here we see them make an existential choice to follow through with their mission, knowing that it will end in death. This choice is the single most important nuance that Stoppard adds to the given dimensions of Shakespeare's text. It does not make tragic heroes of them, for their deaths are still meaningless, but it does give them, at last, a kind of identity. Their choice is what makes it possible for them to be the subject of their own play, for without a crisis—a moment of decision by the protagonist—there is no drama. If, as the Player says in Act 1, "you look on every exit being an entrance somewhere else," then it is consistent with the theatrical metaphor of the play that the exit from life to death is an entrance into the realm of art, which is a kind of immortality.

The Player commands his troupe to show their skills at dying. Still costumed like the members of the Danish court, they perform in dumb show the several deaths at the end of *Hamlet*. Their tableau scene fades into darkness. Then with a whimper, Rosencrantz is snuffed out by darkness, and finally Guildenstern disappears in midsentence. According to the stage directions, "immediately the whole stage is lit up, revealing, upstage, arranged in the approximate positions last held by the dead tragedians, the tableau of court and corpses which is the last scene of *Hamlet*." The two Ambassadors from England report to Horatio, in Shakespeare's words, that "Rosencrantz and Guildenstern are dead."

The roots in *Hamlet* for *Rosencrantz and Guildenstern Are Dead* have been amply indicated. However much Stoppard's play owes to Shakespeare's complex, richly textured tragedy, an equal debt is due to Samuel Beckett's spare, lean, abstract tragicomedy *Waiting for Godot*. Stoppard's influences are not ephemeral ones: the former play is generally acknowledged to be one of the two greatest tragedies of all time (along with Sophocles' *Oedipus Rex*), and the latter has been called the most influential play of the twentieth century. They are, at the very least, the supreme examples of Elizabethan tragedy and of Theatre of the Absurd.

Leonard Powlick has suggested that the switching back and forth of styles in *Rosencrantz and Guildenstern Are Dead*, between Elizabethan tragedy and Theatre of the Absurd, is a conscious artistic statement in itself. When Rosencrantz and Guildenstern read the letter and choose to accept death, they are choosing the higher and more restricting form, tragedy, over a contemporary hybrid form that offers only the insecurity of not knowing. Powlick sees a relationship between their choice and the rationale described in Erich Fromm's

Escape from Freedom: so strong is fear of disorder in many people that they will actually choose to relinquish their freedom in order to live under a repressive dictatorship, which offers the security of an ordered society.[6]

Pursuing this interpretation, one might say that Rosencrantz and Guildenstern's desire to be confined within the ordered system of tragic art is, paradoxically, a function of their small stature. The true tragic hero would attain stature by the substantively monumental scale of his struggle to the death within the restricting matrix of tragic form, but Rosencrantz and Guildenstern do not struggle. They merely allow themselves to disappear. "Death is not anything . . . death is not . . . It's the absence of presence, nothing more . . . the endless time of never coming back . . . a gap you can't see, and when the wind blows through it, it makes no sound. . . . " This is the nonheroic mode of death in an absurd universe.

Theatre of the Absurd was the name given by Martin Esslin[7] to the work of dramatists such as Beckett, Eugene Ionesco, Arthur Adamov, and N.F. Simpson, whose plays reflected the general spiritual malaise of the early 1950s: the cold-war period's fear of nuclear holocaust; a breakdown of interpersonal communication, often attributed to the rise of television; the subordination of human values to rampant materialism. The absurdists dealt with such concerns in a nondidactic manner, by depicting a world already gone out of control, an irrational universe in which there is no linear logic of narrative progression—no traditional beginning, middle, and end. Objects take on as much life or significance as characters. The protagonist is no longer a "hero," but a cipher. Language is often nonsensical or otherwise devalued.

Rosencrantz and Guildenstern Are Dead, which appeared more than ten years after the peak of the so-called absurdist movement, bears traces of these general characteristics. The structure of the play is imposed from without; that is, the two "nonheroes" merely drift within the preexisting structure of *Hamlet*. In the earliest published version of the play (London, May 1967), a circular structure was used: a new pair of attendant lords was summoned, apparently to reenact the same story from the beginning. This ending was cut during rehearsals at the National Theatre.[8] By then, even Ionesco had abandoned this cliché of the Theatre of the Absurd. The coin is the most recurrent object in the play, and it seems to obey the laws of chance of a universe apart. The breakdown of language occurs in a number of passages such as the following:

> PLAYER: Why?
> GUIL: Ah. (*To* ROS:) Why?
> ROS: Exactly.
> GUIL: Exactly what?
> ROS: Exactly why?
> GUIL: Exactly why *what*?
> ROS: What?
> GUIL: *Why*?
> ROS: Why what, exactly?
> GUIL: Why is he mad?
> ROS: *I* don't know!

Despite such affinities with the Theatre of the Absurd, Stoppard is not an absurdist at heart. The metaphysical anguish expressed in *Rosencrantz and Guildenstern Are Dead* is really only a literary/ philosophical exercise, not a profound vision of the universe. He is, however, a genuine admirer of Samuel Beckett, from whose *Waiting for Godot* his play has derived so many specific traits, some of which are discussed in Robert Brustein's review, "Waiting for Hamlet,"[9] and in Anthony Callen's article, "Stoppard's Godot."[10] Stoppard himself has said:

Waiting for Godot—there's just no telling what sort of effect it had on our society, who wrote because of it, or wrote in a different way because of it. But it really redefined the minima of theatrical experience. Up to then you had to have X; suddenly you had X minus one.

Of course, it would be absurd to deny my enormous debt to it, and love for it. To me the representative attitude is "I am a human nothing." Beckett qualifies as he goes along. He picks up a proposition and then dismantles and qualifies each part of its structure as he goes along, until he nullifies what he started out with. Beckett gives me more pleasure than I can express because he always ends up with a man surrounded by the wreckage of a proposition he had made in confidence only two minutes before.[11]

Waiting for Godot places two tramps, Vladimir and Estragon, on a featureless road to nowhere. They have been told to wait for Godot, but they do not know who Godot is, or why they must wait. The action of the play consists of what they do to pass the time while waiting: chatting, telling stories, discussing suicide, and toying with such objects as a boot or a carrot. In each of the two acts, they are briefly distracted by a meeting with Pozzo and Lucky, whose movement on the road, unlike their own, seems to have direction and purpose. At the end of each act, a boy arrives to tell Vladimir and Estragon that Godot will not come today, but will come tomorrow. They say to each other: "Well? Shall we go?" "Yes, let's go." But they do not move.

Like Vladimir and Estragon, Rosencrantz and Guildenstern are mutually dependent and inseparable. Both pairs are "little men," insignificant people, waiting for something to change their mode of existence. Both pairs are on the road because a messenger summoned them, without explanation. The Player serves to distract Rosencrantz and Guildenstern from their boredom and confusion, much as Pozzo and Lucky do for Beckett's duo. In Act 2, Rosencrantz tells three pointless stories in succession, and, similarly, in *Waiting for Godot*, the more childish tramp, Estragon, is the storyteller. Callen points out that it is Rosencrantz "who would prefer the Players' sexual performance whereas his partner wants a serious play, just as Estragon wants Lucky to dance whereas his partner wants him to think. Appropriately enough, Rosencrantz, like Estragon, is the one to have his trousers fall down."[12] When conversation bogs down, Vladimir says, "Come on, Gogo, return the ball, can't you, once in a way," and, similarly, Guildenstern says to Rosencrantz, "Why don't you say something original! No wonder the whole thing is so stagnant!"

There are also striking parallels in the comic business of both plays, such as when Rosencrantz and Guildenstern snatch the letter back and forth in Act 3, reminding one of the passing of hats from one head to another in *Waiting for Godot*. The following exchange in Stoppard's play evokes one of Vladimir and Estragon's recurrent preoccupations:

> Ros: Well, shall we stretch our legs?
> Guil: I don't feel like stretching my legs.
> Ros: I'll stretch them for you, if you like.
> Guil: No.
> Ros: We could stretch each other's. That way we wouldn't have to go anywhere.

In another instance, when Rosencrantz and Guildenstern are waiting to see Hamlet in Act 2, they seem to echo the central thought of *Waiting for Godot*:

> *Guil marches down to join Ros. They stand still for a moment in their original positions.*
>
> Guil: Well, at last we're getting somewhere.
>
> *Pause.*
>
> Of course, he might not come.

In addition to the influence of Beckett that Stoppard so readily acknowledges, there are obvious resemblances to Luigi Pirandello's *Six Characters in Search of an Author* (1921). Stoppard told Giles Gordon in 1968 that he had not been conscious of Pirandello's influence on his work: "I know very little about him, I'm afraid. I've seen very little and I really wasn't aware of that as an influence."[13] He conceded, however, that it would be difficult for anyone to write a play today that did not contain some legacy from Pirandello. Consciously or not, much of modern theater has been shaped by the revolutionary arrival on stage of those six characters who had been created only in an artist's imagination and were thus endowed with substance but not with form. Like Rosencrantz and Guildenstern, they needed a structure in which to prove to themselves that they existed.

Pirandello's preoccupation with the notion of the relativity of truth recurs throughout Stoppard's canon. One of Stoppard's favorite comedic and structural devices, for example, is to present a situation that seems fantastic or preposterous at first glance, but which makes complete sense when the surrounding circumstances are revealed to certain characters and to the audience. A number of statements about our inability to pin down and define reality may be found in *Rosencrantz and Guildenstern Are Dead*, but perhaps the most succinctly evocative of these is a line spoken by Guildenstern in Act 2: "A Chinaman of the T'ang Dynasty—and, by which definition, a philosopher— dreamed he was a butterfly, and from that moment he was never quite sure that he was not a butterfly dreaming it was a Chinese philosopher."

Theater-within-the-theater is a device used by both Pirandello and Stoppard to examine the relationship of art and life, or, in the words of Pirandello's preface to *Six Characters in Search of an Author*, "the inherent tragic conflict between life (which is always moving and changing) and form (which fixes it, immutable)."[14] We have seen that the primary conflict in *Rosencrantz and Guildenstern Are Dead* is the pair's struggle to "move and change" in order to make sense of their own lives, an impossible feat, since the main outlines of their existence are predetermined by the fixed form of Shakespeare's *Hamlet*. The tragedians serve as coordinates for the audience between the structured world of Hamlet's story (art) and the void (life) in which Rosencrantz and Guildenstern must operate. In *Six Characters in Search of an Author*, the six characters, who belong to a limbo between illusion and reality, are pitted against the Manager, his Leading Lady, and other members of his theatrical company, whose own struggle to create a theatrical illusion of reality proves to be a vain endeavor. In both works, the play-within-the-play structure allows tensions to develop between the characters as they were originally conceived and the new frame of reference in which they are placed.

Another feature of Pirandello's work is his exploration of the multiplicity of the human personality, the idea that one person may don a variety of masks to face different aspects of reality. We have noted the identity problems of Rosencrantz and Guildenstern, as well as Stoppard's assertion that his protagonists are actually two facets of the same personality. The following passage is one example from *Rosencrantz and Guildenstern Are Dead*, of the kind of philosophical thought that Pirandello made germane to modern drama:

GUIL: . . . Nor did we come all this way for a christening. All *that*—preceded us. But we are comparatively fortunate; we might have been left to sift the whole field of human nomenclature, like two blind men looting a bazaar for their own portraits. . . . At least we are presented with alternatives.

ROS: Well as from now—

GUIL: —But not choice.

ROS: You made me look ridiculous in there.

GUIL: I looked just as ridiculous as you did.

ROS (*an anguished cry*): Consistency is all I ask!

GUIL (*low, wry rhetoric*): Give us this day our daily mask.

Although Rosencrantz and Guildenstern indulge in a fair amount of role-playing or, figuratively speaking, trying on different masks for each other's amusement, they are not themselves fully rounded characters. They are weakly motivated, express few opinions, have no memories or hopes, experience no strong emotion, and fail to interrelate meaningfully with other characters. The lack of characterization was certainly a conscious artistic choice on Stoppard's part, a choice that was intrinsic to the absurdist mode, as well as compatible with his own early aversion to expressing emotion in his writing.

Since Rosencrantz and Guildenstern are the protagonists of a full-length play, however, it is essential that they be perceived by the audience as sympathetic. As long as they remain faceless ciphers, rather than characters with human complexity, though, it is hard to muster more than some detached compassion for their general plight. "I like them as people," Stoppard has said,[15] but whatever likeable qualities he imagines in them do not come across in the text itself. This limitation on the script as literature can be overcome in performance by actors who bring to the stage life of the two nonentities the nuance and sparkle of individual personalities.

What Stoppard did for Rosencrantz and Guildenstern as characters was to eliminate Hamlet's suspicion that they are acting in league with Claudius. Shakespeare leaves ambiguous the true nature of their involvement in the court intrigue. Many critics—and directors of productions of *Hamlet*—have assumed that, if Hamlet sees them as conspiratorial opportunists who would betray a friendship, they must be so. In fact, Robert Brustein and John Weightman have both suggested that Stoppard omitted their "recorders" scene because it would "expose" Rosencrantz and Guildenstern as spies for Claudius.[16] This supposition is quite unfounded. When Stoppard set out to portray them as "a couple of bewildered innocents rather than a couple of henchmen,"[17] he did not violate Shakespeare's limited depiction of Rosencrantz and Guildenstern except to ignore Hamlet's personal and perhaps crazed perception of their disloyalty.

There is one instance of character evolvement in Stoppard's play. It is a very minor one, considering that the stuff of drama is change and the acquisition of insight. Early in the play Guildenstern tends to question the way things are. Faced with the impossible run of heads in the coin-toss game, for example, the stage direction tells us that "Guildenstern is well alive to the oddity of it. He's not worried about the money, but he is worried by the implications; aware but not going to panic about it—his character note." By Act 3, Guildenstern has changed, to the extent that he can say: "I've lost all capacity for disbelief. I'm not sure that I could even rise to a little gentle scepticism." It must be noted that this is not a positive evolvement toward increased awareness, but rather an erosion of what little there was to distinguish his personality from that of Rosencrantz.

One is tempted to assume that Stoppard's avoidance of psychological motivation and of a realistic narrative line was intended to insure that the spectator not get caught up in a human drama, but instead participate in an intellectual exercise, a philosophical exploration—for this is indeed what happens when the play is performed. A decade after writing *Rosencrantz and Guildenstern Are Dead*, Stoppard seemed to disavow such an interpretation of his intentions. He told Jon Bradshaw (*New York*, January 10, 1977):

The play had no substance beyond its own terms, beyond its apparent situation. It was about two courtiers in a castle. Two nonentities surrounded by intrigue, given very little information and much of that false. It had nothing to do with the condition of modern man or the decline of metaphysics. One wasn't thinking, "Life is an anteroom in which one has to kill time." Or I wasn't, at any rate. . . . But *Rosencrantz and Guildenstern* wasn't about that at all. It was about two blokes, right?

In a lecture at the University of California at Santa Barbara in January 1977, Stoppard admitted that some idea content might be found lurking beneath the surface:

Whenever I talk to intelligent students about my work, I feel nervous, as if I were going through customs. "Anything to declare, sir?" "Not really, just two chaps sitting in a castle at Elsinore, playing games, that's all." "Then let's have a look in your suitcase, if you don't mind, sir." And, sure enough, under the first layer of shirts there's a pound of hash and fifty watches and all kinds of exotic contraband. "How do you explain this, sir?" "I'm sorry, Officer, I admit it's there, but I honestly can't remember packing it."[18]

"It would be fatal to set out to write primarily on an intellectual level," Stoppard said to Tom Prideaux in 1968. "Instead one writes about human beings under stress—whether it is about losing one's trousers or being nailed to the cross."[19] Yet Stoppard has asserted on another occasion—as we have observed—that "it doesn't interest me in any way to create *characters*."[20] It is debatable whether, without creating characters, it is possible to write about human beings under stress.

Rosencrantz and Guildenstern Are Dead is a flawed play, although not as seriously flawed as one would surmise from C. O. Gardner's opinion that "the 'despair' and the 'absurdity' are of the strictly fashionable variety, and that the thing is in fact a swill, composed of second-hand Beckett, third-hand Kafka, and the goon show, with casual sprinklings of Chaplinesque pathos, logical-positivist shadow-boxing, Pinterian 'grimness,' and so on."[21]

Despite its reliance on literary borrowings and its lack of human values with which an audience can empathize, the play's most serious problem is its frequent lapses into exchanges such as the following:

> GUIL: Well . . .
>
> ROS: Quite . . .
>
> GUIL: Well, well.
>
> ROS: Quite, quite. (*Nods with spurious confidence.*) Seek him out. (*Pause.*) Etcetera.
>
> GUIL: Quite.
>
> ROS: Well. (*Small pause.*) Well, that's a step in the right direction.
>
> GUIL: You didn't like him?
>
> ROS: Who?
>
> GUIL: Good God, I hope more tears are shed for *us*! . . .
>
> ROS: Well, it's *progress*, isn't it? Something positive. Seek him out. (*Looks round without moving his feet.*) Where does one begin . . . ? (*Takes one step toward the wings and halts.*)
>
> GUIL: Well, that's a step in the right direction.

These dialogue sequences convey by their very lack of color or movement the intended sense of existential anguish, but they dissipate the tension needed to sustain interest. The conflict that keeps the play going is not dynamic, since the protagonists do not take action but are merely acted upon. This problem is magnified by the length of the play, which can run as long as three hours.

Although the play's faults are a matter of opinion, it is a matter of fact that *Rosencrantz and Guildenstern Are Dead* was a "hit" in London and New York, and that within a decade it had over 250 productions in twenty languages. The play pleases its audiences primarily because it is funny; there is enough good comedy to carry the audience's approval over the dull passages. A good director can even camouflage those loosely written sections by rapid pacing and by the inventive use of physical comedy. Most importantly, the director must avoid taking the play too seriously. Giving weight to the rather thin philosophical content is the one sure path to disaster in a production of this play. A similar problem was often encountered by Jean-Paul Sartre's *No Exit*, written in 1944, but frequently produced in the 1950s when existentialism flourished as a critical perspective. Too many directors zeroed in on the existentialist philosophical context of the play and overstressed it, but *No Exit* excites the imagination in a theatrical context only when it is approached as a story about three incompatible people confined to a hotel room. Stoppard may well have been hoping to forestall such directorial pitfalls when he told interviewers that, in *Rosencrantz and Guildenstern Are Dead*, he was just writing "about two blokes. . . ."

Some of the most profound expressions of appreciation for *Rosencrantz and Guildenstern Are Dead* have come from actors who have performed in it. Robert Egan's performance of the Player's role at the Alabama Shakespeare Festival in 1977 led him to publish a scholarly analysis of the play in *Theatre Journal*.[22] John Wood, Guildenstern in the New York production that opened in October 1967, has voiced his admiration for several of Stoppard's plays. He has said that "the plays are a great deal more difficult than we think. I rehearsed *Rosencrantz and Guildenstern* for six weeks, toured for three and played for three months before I was able to hold the whole pattern in my head at one time."[23]

Indeed, it is in performance that the play may be most fairly and favorably judged. The flaws that have been perceived in it when it is evaluated by conventional literary criticism prove elusive when a given production is analyzed. *Rosencrantz and Guildenstern*

Are Dead was not primarily conceived as a literary artifact, but as a blueprint for theatrical interpretation. In performance its aesthetic conceits and strings of apparent non sequiturs can achieve a curiously dynamic harmony by the integration of audience responses. Dialogue passages that seem either ponderous or meaningless on the printed page acquire dramatic significance when spoken to reveal their complex and stunning rhythmic patterns. Endowed with individual actors' gestures, inflections, and presence, the featureless characters do become real people who can elicit an audience's involvement on a human plane. Stoppard had undertaken to provide a satisfying evening's entertainment for a broad spectrum of theatergoers, and to do so without underrating that audience's intelligence. In both respects, he was—with *Rosencrantz and Guidenstern Are Dead*—"home free."

3

Magister Ludi:
Jumpers **and** *Travesties*

"I write plays because dialogue is the most respectable way of contradicting myself."[1] This is one of the most frequently quoted of Stoppard's epigrammatic remarks to interviewers, and the truth of it is nowhere better illustrated than in his two major full-length plays, *Jumpers* (1972) and *Travesties* (1974). Both works are so dense with contradictory ideas that the audience member comes away from the evening's entertainment having learned—or been intellectually stimulated—at least as much as if he had attended a debate instead of a play. This is not, of course, Stoppard's primary intention, for he realizes that the audience "will not be kept in its seats by Ideas,"[2] nor is it, ultimately, a defect. With these two plays, Stoppard fully mastered the art of the stage. The idea content is theatrically acceptable, even exciting, because it is so skillfully integrated with other elements of drama, and balanced by a highly developed sense of stage values.

It is appropriate to begin by establishing how significant the thought content is in these two plays, since Stoppard's stated aim was to contrive "the perfect marriage between the play of ideas and farce or perhaps even high comedy."[3] Stoppard has repeatedly stressed the view that "a play is not the end product of an idea; the idea is the end product of the play."[4] If one sets out to write with the intention of propounding an idea, the resulting play will be too pat and reductionist. His concern is rather to offer a satisfying evening of theater and to let each member of the audience draw his own conclusions about the ideas presented.

Stoppard's refusal to force an issue in these plays is also a consequence of his method of work. He has said, "My plays are a lot to do with the fact that *I just don't know.*"[5] Although the ideas as such do not determine the outcome of the play, Stoppard's process of coming to grips with what he doesn't know—that is, of examining the fruits of his research from opposing points of view in alternation—seems to serve as a structuring device for the plot, by creating the illusion of forces in conflict.

In preparing to write *Jumpers*, Stoppard set up for himself a crash course of philosophical readings. For *Travesties*, he studied the Dada movement in art and the writings of Lenin and James Joyce. He formed opinions about what he learned, but he let the needs of the play and its characters, rather than his own bias, determine which side would come out on top in terms of the audience's sympathies. Thus, in *Jumpers*, the protagonist George Moore, who happens to express Stoppard's own point of view, loses his argument intellectually but, as the bumbling underdog, keeps us emotionally on his side. In *Travesties*, James Joyce most nearly embodies Stoppard's own attitudes about art, but it is the raffish Tristan Tzara who wins our affection.

Stoppard believes that the most valuable element in his work is "the one that other people are put off by—that is, that there is very often *no* simple, clear statement in my plays. What there is, is a series of conflicting statements made by conflicting characters, and they tend to play a sort of infinite leap-frog. You know, an argument, a refutation, then a rebuttal of the refutation, then a counter-rebuttal, so that there is never any point in this intellectual leap-frog at which I feel *that* is the speech to stop it on, *that* is the last word."[6] Although this method is almost second nature to him, he has said that "*Jumpers* was the first play in which I specifically set out to ask a question and try to answer it, or at any rate put the counter question."[7] Dialectical thought provides some impetus for advancing the action in *Jumpers,* but it is the externalization of that thought in theatrical images that makes this play the supreme dramatic achievement in Stoppard's canon to date. *Travesties* repeats the pattern, and falls only a little short of that mark as a piece of writing, although it may have an edge over *Jumpers* in the theater. It was selected by *Time* as one of the ten best plays of the decade.[8]

The intellectual argument in *Jumpers* pits moral philosophy against logical positivism. The moral view of the universe (upheld by the play's protagonist George Moore) is based upon absolute standards of what constitutes good and evil. Moore's precepts are valid, but it is the means by which he tries to illustrate those precepts that fail him. For example, his use of logic to validate his faith in God—which ultimately must be taken "on faith"—serves him no better than his choice of illustrative realia for his lecture: a tortoise, a hare, a bow and arrows. The logical positivists outnumber George, objectifying Stoppard's view that most of modern society tends to rationalize human behavior through pragmatic considerations. Their view, in the words of the play, is that "good and evil aren't actually *good* or *bad* in any absolute or metaphysical sense," but are "social and psychological conventions which we have evolved in order to make living in groups a practical possibility." This view allows one "to conclude that telling lies is not *sinful* but simply antisocial." The mental acrobatics needed to justify this relativistic philosophy are cunningly externalized in the theatrical image of the team of university philosophy professors-cum-gymnasts who, under the direction of Sir Archibald Jumper, Vice-Chancellor of the university, form human pyramids on stage.

Jumpers begins with blackout sketches of three different kinds of entertainment, whose full context is only gradually made clear during the course of the play. Dorothy Moore, introduced by an unseen announcer as a "much-missed, much-loved star of the musical stage," tries to sing "Shine On Harvest Moon," but is unable to continue. We learn much later that, ever since British astronauts landed on the moon, she has lost her capacity to romanticize it in song, and this has brought about her mental breakdown. If Dotty is seen as the sensitive artist who cannot create on cue, the next performer represents her opposite: the cheap entertainer pandering to the lowest level of taste. The latter is a woman swinging in and out of a spotlight on a chandelier, as she strips off her clothing. Just when she appears quite naked, a cocktail waiter walks into the path of her swing and is knocked off his feet in slapstick comedy style, to the sound of breaking glass.

The third snatch of entertainment is the performance of eight middle-aged gymnasts in yellow athletic suits. Introduced as the "INCREDIBLE—RADICAL!—LIBERAL!—JUMPERS!!," They might be said to suggest the measures necessary to popularize political and intellectual ideas. When George Moore enters during this gymnastic display, to complain of the noise, we realize that all these events are occurring at a party in George and Dotty Moore's house. George has been trying to get some work done in his study while Dotty is hostess for the Radical Liberals' celebration of victory in the recent election.

The Jumpers form a human pyramid, by which Dotty is hidden from view. There is a gunshot, and one Jumper from the bottom row is "blown out of the pyramid." Dotty walks through the gap to where the shot Jumper lies. The stage image is vivid:

He starts to move, dying, pulling himself up against DOTTY's legs. She looks at him in surprise as he crawls up her body. His blood is on her dress. She holds him under his arms, and looks around in a bewildered way. . . . The pyramid has been defying gravity for these few seconds. Now it slowly collapses into the dark, imploding on the missing part, and rolling and separating, out of sight . . .

Dotty whimpers to someone named Archie, who, unseen, tells her to "just keep him out of sight until morning. I'll be back." Suddenly the study, hall, and bedroom of the Moores' apartment become visible. George is shuffling papers in the study. In the bedroom, Dotty, still supporting the corpse, is distracted by what she sees on television. A news commentator announces that after the discovery of damage to the British rocket that limited its capacity for the return trip, the two astronauts had fought over which of them would get to go. Television viewers watched Commanding Officer Scott knock Astronaut Oates to the ground and leave him standing forlornly on the lunar surface. Flipping channels by remote control, Dotty alternately sees a commercial advertisement and a political victory procession with military music. A parallel between Dotty's nervous disorder and the chaos of modern life is thus effectively established.

The noisy arrivals of the apartment building's maintenance man Crouch (the cocktail waiter at the party) and of George's Secretary (the stripper on the chandelier) indicate to Dotty that it is morning already. She takes off her bloodied dress and softly calls for help. The bedroom blacks out, and the focus shifts to George's study, where he begins dictating to his Secretary the lecture he will give that evening. George's long monologue, interspersed by Dotty's calls from offstage, reveals his mental clumsiness and begins the polemical aspect of the play.

Stoppard's audacity in incorporating this early in the play what is virtually a ten- to fifteen-minute philosophical treatise (in a lightly satirical vein) is compensated by his own awareness of the problem posed in the theater. He indicates this with George's line: "Experience has taught me that to attempt to sustain the attention of rival schools of academics by argument alone is tantamount to constructing a Gothic arch out of junket." The solution for both Stoppard and George is to introduce an apparently illogical visual aid. George sets up an archery target on his daybed and notches an arrow into his bow, all the while discoursing on infinite series as proof of the existence of God. ("Since an arrow shot towards a target first had to cover half the distance, and then half the remainder, and then half the remainder after that, and so on *ad infinitum,* the result was, as I will now demonstrate, that though an arrow is always approaching its target, it never quite gets there, and Saint Sebastian died of fright." Dotty chooses this moment to top her earlier cries of "Murder!," "Rape!," and "Wolves!," with the cry, *"Fire!"* George is thus startled into letting his arrow fly. It disappears over the top of the wardrobe.

Undaunted, George continues to expound his theories. The military music from Dotty's television begins to build under his speech. Finally, "by way of regaining your attention," he takes a live tortoise from a box. He then opens a second box, in which he keeps a live hare, but this box is empty. He searches the study, calling for Thumper, then crosses to the bedroom with the tortoise under one arm. When the bedroom lights come up, the Jumper's corpse is nowhere in sight, but Dotty's nude body is sprawled across the bed. George sees that she is playing charades—acting out a proverb or a book title. He readily guesses *The Naked and the*

Dead, although he does not see the dead Jumper that makes the latter half of the title more pointed. It will be seen in Dotty and George's scenes together that the structured format of games is the framework in which their marriage subsists most comfortably.

Dotty pleads with George to stay with her and reproaches him for not being one to help her out of a tight spot, as Archie would. George is unhappy that Archie, his Vice-Chancellor, has been paying daily visits to Dotty in her bedroom, but Dotty reminds him that Archie is a qualified psychiatrist who keeps her spirits up. George and Dotty become nostalgic about how they met when she was a student in his class and how their "tutorials descended, from the metaphysical to the merely physical . . . not so much down to earth as down to the carpet." His career had never accelerated, and he never wrote his book, whereas Dotty, despite all her insecurities, was able to become a singing star and to charm the likes of Bertrand Russell and Sir Archibald Jumper.

Dotty apparently hopes to get their interaction back inside the comfortable parameters of a game. She empties the goldfish bowl in the bathtub, puts it over her head like a space helmet, moves about the room like a moonwalker and mimes picking up a small coin. "The Moon and Sixpence," George immediately guesses, and then he begins to fulminate on political theory. In this field, too, Dotty has an edge over George. She informs him of the latest turn of current events: with the Radical Liberal election victory, the Church is to be "rationalized" like the railways. The Archbishop of Canterbury is to be a political appointment, and the new appointee is Sam Clegthorpe, the former Radical Liberal spokesman for Agriculture, and an agnostic.

The disorder of the times is dexterously evoked in a rush of puns and epigrams, and by visual images combining the television picture and George's description of what he sees from the window:

> GEORGE: . . . Credibility is an expanding field. . . .
> Sheer disbelief hardly registers on the face before the head is
> nodding with all the wisdom of instant hindsight. 'Archbishop
> Clegthorpe? Of course! The inevitable capstone to a career in
> veterinary medicine!' What happened to the old Archbishop?
> DOTTY: He abdicated . . . or resigned or uncoped
> himself—
> GEORGE (*thoughtfully*): Dis-mantled himself, perhaps.
>
> (*Dotty turns on the TV: the Moon.*)

Good   God!   (*At   window.*)   I   can   actually   *see*
Clegthorpe!—marching along, attended by two chaplains in
belted raincoats.

> DOTTY: Is he wearing a mitre?
> GEORGE: Yes. He's blessing people to right and left. He
> must be drunk. (*He stares out the window. Dotty stares at the
> TV.*)
> DOTTY: Poor moon man, falling home like Lucifer. (*She
> turns off the TV: Screen goes white.*) . . . Of course, to some-
> body *on* it, the moon is always full, so the local idea of a sane
> action may well differ from ours.

This last, incidental statement of Dotty's is an apt
summary of Stoppard's essential dramatic vision, which
depicts a situation that appears totally absurd to the
uninitiated but that makes perfect sense when it is seen
from the right vantage point. An example of this device
occurs at the end of George and Dotty's scene, when he
answers the doorbell "holding a bow-and-arrow in one
hand and a tortoise in the other, his face covered in
shaving foam." This is a startling vision to the man at
the door, but quite natural from the audience's point of
view.

The philosophical polemic is resumed when
Dotty, in the course of telling George what "Archie
says," articulates some logical positivist principles.
George's moralistic response spoken in the heat of pas-
sion makes much more sense here than it did when he

laboriously developed a proof in the pompously sterile context of his lecture. When Dotty tells him that Archie considers the Church "a monument to irrationality," George replies:

The National Gallery is a monument to irrationality!— and so is a nicely kept garden, or a lover's favor, or a home for stray dogs! You stupid woman, if rationality were the criterion for things being allowed to exist, the world would be one gigantic field of soya beans! . . . The irrational, the emotional, the whimsical . . . these are the stamp of humanity which makes reason a civilizing force.

Exasperated by his failure to find Thumper and by Dotty's querulousness, George is about to get back to work on his lecture when the doorbell rings. It is Inspector Bones, who has come to investigate a telephone call reporting events that may have occurred in the Moores' apartment the previous evening. Bones carries a bunch of flowers to present to Dotty—his favorite singer—in the event that he does not find it necessary to arrest her. George tells Bones that he had called the police himself to complain, anonymously, about the noise coming from his own apartment, because he was having trouble with his paper and "anticipated a strongly argued riposte from Professor McFee, who obviously thought he had the matter well in hand since he was one of the people actually making all the noise." Questioned closely about McFee, George explains that McFee, a Professor of Logic who doesn't believe in good and bad as such, "is to be his chief adversary at the symposium that evening." George mistakes Bones's obvious interest in McFee for a fascination with philosophy, even after Bones hints at murder and asks to see the "scene of the crime."

Bones goes to look in the kitchen for a vase for his flowers. George goes to tell Dotty of Bones's visit, but they talk at cross-purposes, because she thinks he knows all about the shooting of "poor Duncan McFee," whose body hangs, hidden from George's view, on the back of the door. Bones gets to meet Dotty in person, and his subjective reaction is conveyed through romanticized lighting and music in the bedroom, while he stands gazing speechlessly at her. The focus shifts back to the study, where George delivers three more pages of his lecture, a passage that attempts to discredit the relativist approach to aesthetics. A blast of music from one of Dotty's recordings draws George out to the hall. Bones, too, enters the hall. They confer inaudibly under the music and exit together to the kitchen.

At this juncture, Archie enters stealthily by the front door. He is "an impressive figure, exquisitely dressed: orchid in button hole, cigarette in long black holder, and everything which those details suggest." After verifying that the coast is clear, he beckons to seven Jumpers in yellow track suits. They set up some television equipment in the bedroom, stuff the corpse into a large plastic bag, and exit smoothly on the last beat of the song. Act 1 ends with Dotty and Archie alone in the bedroom.

When Act 2 begins, Bones is on his way to Dotty's bedroom, pushing a tea trolley with dinner and wine for two. He pauses to discuss Dotty's situation with George, and this time the two men talk at crosspurposes. Without being explicit, Bones hints that George should employ a psychiatrist to testify that Dotty was insane when she killed McFee. George, still unaware that Bones is investigating anything more than an anonymous phone call complaining of too much noise, claims responsibility for whatever happens in his own house.

BONES: I don't think the burden of being a householder extends to responsibility for any crime committed in the premises.

GEORGE: Crime? You call that a crime?

BONES (*with more heat*): Well, what would you call it?

GEORGE: It was just a bit of *fun*! Where's your sense of humor, man?

BONES (*staggered*): I don't know, you bloody philosophers are all the same, aren't you? A man is dead and you're as cool as you like. Your wife begged me with tears in her eyes to go easy on you, and I don't mind admitting I was deeply moved—

GEORGE: Excuse me—

BONES: (*angrily*): But you're wasted on her, mate. What on earth made *her* marry *you*, I'll never know, when there are so many better men—decent, strong, protective, understanding, sensitive—

GEORGE: Did you say somebody was dead?

BONES: Stone dead, in the bedroom.

GEORGE: Don't be ridiculous.

BONES: The body is lying on the floor!

GEORGE (*going to door*): You have obviously taken leave of your senses.

BONES: Don't touch it!—it will have to be examined for fingerprints.

GEORGE: If there is a body on the floor, it will have my *footprints* on it.

The corpse is, of course, gone from the bedroom, but Archie is there, playing charades with Dotty. George retreats to his study to resume work.

Bones, jealous of the newcomer's intimacy with Dotty, begins to interrogate Archie, who—we now learn—is, besides being Vice-Chancellor of George's university, "a doctor of medicine, philosophy, literature and law, with diplomas in psychological medicine and P.T. including gym." Archie quickly takes command of the situation. He gives the first complete explanation of the incident we witnessed early in the play:

The plain facts are that while performing some modest acrobatics for the entertainment of Miss Moore's party guests, Professor McFee was killed by a bullet fired from the outer darkness. We all saw him shot, but none of us saw who shot him. With the possible exception of McFee's fellow gymnasts, anybody could have fired the shot, and anybody could have had a reason for doing so, including, incidentally, myself.

Archie's possible motive would have proceeded from McFee's precipitous decision, brought about by the spectacle of the astronauts fighting on the moon, to abandon the logical positivist philosophy, of which he had been "the guardian and figurehead," and to move into the opposite camp—that of George Moore and moral philosophy. Archie then tells Bones that McFee's body has been found in the park "by some gymnasts on an early morning keep-fit run" and suggests that they collaborate on the theory that "McFee, suffering from nervous strain brought on by the appalling pressure of overwork . . . left here last night in a mood of deep depression, and wandered into the park, where he crawled into a large plastic bag and shot himself. . . ." A few moments later, Archie tells the same story to George:

> ARCHIE: . . . McFee's dead.
> GEORGE: What?!!
> ARCHIE: Shot himself this morning, in the park, in a plastic bag.
> GEORGE: My God! Why?
> ARCHIE: It's hard to say. He was always tidy.

However, George is not aware that McFee had converted to moral philosophy:

> GEORGE: . . . Where did he find the despair . . . ? I thought the whole *point* of denying the Absolute was to reduce the scale, instantly, to the inconsequential behavior of inconsequential animals; that nothing could ever be that important . . .
> ARCHIE: Including, I suppose, death. . . . It's an interesting view of atheism, as a sort of *crutch* for those who can't bear the reality of God. . .

Archie tells George that the symposium will take place that evening, as scheduled, and that, in the debate, he himself will represent the logical positivist position that McFee was to have taken. He does not mention McFee's change of heart.

George's musings on the subject of death are reminiscent of those of Rosencrantz and Guildenstern in Stoppard's earlier play. His confusion over whether or not Archie is having an affair with Dotty, as appearances would lead him to believe, echoes a similar dilemma faced by Mr Moon in Stoppard's 1966 novel *Lord Malquist and Mr Moon*. Archie's clinical appraisal of Dotty as his psychiatric patient is full of double entendres and sensual imagery. When Archie leaves him, George can only agonize, "How the hell does one know what to believe?" and then drown his baser thoughts in philosophy again.

Archie crosses to the bedroom and follows up a previous attempt to bribe Bones to abandon the investigation by insinuating that Bones's presence in the bedroom alone with Dotty, who is sobbing on the bed, would suffice to bring "a tragic end to an incorruptible career." Bones disappears from the play, his murder mystery still unsolved.

Stoppard makes skillful use of verbal cues to motivate a new train of thought and a shift in visual focus on the stage. An example of this is George's sudden realization, as he prepares his lecture, that "McFee jumped and left nothing behind but a vacancy." George's philosophical point is that McFee's denial of God's existence meant that his death was an uncluttered completion of his philosophy, leaving no trail of unanswered metaphysical speculations. The audience, however, is reminded of the visual image of vacancy in the gymnasts' pyramid when McFee was shot. Finally, George, who still knows nothing of that occurrence, objectifies the literal meaning of his words: McFee's death also leaves the prestigious Chair of Logic vacant for a new appointment. George crosses to the bedroom to ask if he, as a senior professor of philosophy, might be considered for the chair.

He finds Archie and Dotty dining from the tea trolley, while Archie makes a show of conducting a consultation. Although his request is brushed aside, George becomes enraged only upon discovery that the goldfish died when Dotty emptied the fishbowl into the bathtub for her earlier game of charades. Dotty responds to his anger with an eloquent evocation of the reason for her nervous breakdown:

Man is on the Moon, his feet on solid ground, and he has seen us whole, all in one go, *little, local* . . . and all our absolutes, the thou-shalts and the thou-shalt-nots that seemed to be the very condition of our existence, how did *they* look to two moonmen with a single neck to save between them? Like the local customs of another place. When that thought drips through to the bottom, people won't just carry on. There is going to be such . . . breakage, such gnashing of unclean meat, such covetting of neighbours' oxen and knowing of neighbours' wives, such dishonourings of mothers and fathers, and bowings and scrapings to images graven and incarnate, such killing of goldfish and maybe more—(*Looks up, tear-stained.*) Because the truths that have been taken on trust, they've never had edges before, there was no vantage point to stand on and see where they stopped. (*And weeps.*)

The moment is ambiguous. This may or may not be Dotty's confession of having killed McFee.

George apparently latches onto the idea that, if Dotty murdered the goldfish, she might also have murdered Thumper, to make the casserole she and Archie are eating. This thought is on George's mind when Crouch arrives by the front door to follow up on the shooting of Duncan McFee, which had occurred when he was "doing the drinks." When George, referring to Thumper, says, "Do you realize she's in there now, *eating* him?," Crouch assumes that Dotty's condition has worsened to the point that she would dine on McFee's corpse. At last George comes to the realization that McFee died not inside a plastic bag in the park, but in this apartment, and that Dotty is implicated as the murderess.

He strides back into the bedroom, this time to discover that Dotty and Archie are hidden from view by the curtains drawn around the bed. Here Stoppard employs again his familiar device of setting up a situation for which the most obvious apparent explanation is the wrong one. George's first assumption is that Archie must be having an affair with Dotty, and he further surmises that, if Dotty was capable of killing, cooking, and eating Thumper, she must also have killed McFee. But Archie emerges to explain that he is examining Dotty and that the television camera poking its lens through the bed curtains is a light-sensitive dermatograph taking sensory readings of Dotty's skin. In production, the texture of Dotty's naked skin magnified on the television screen resembled the surface of the moon that had been televised earlier.

George returns to the study, and Archie follows. They find that Crouch is reading George's typescript and articulating a rebuttal of it. Archie is impressed enough to question Crouch about his knowledge of philosophy, which is so unusual in a maintenance man. Crouch explains that philosophy is only a hobby he picked up from conversing with poor Duncan McFee when McFee used to arrive early to pick up his girl, Moore's Secretary. McFee and the Secretary had been secretly betrothed for three years, but he had been about to break off with her as a result of the change in his philosophical views, and to go into a monastery. Thus, the Secretary, too, had a motive for killing McFee. Still, Archie says, as he and Crouch leave the apartment, "The truth to us philosophers, Mr Crouch, is always an interim judgment. We will never even know for certain who did shoot McFee. Unlike mystery novels, life does not guarantee a denouement; and if it came, how would one know whether to believe it?"

Meanwhile, the Secretary has been preparing to leave for her lunch break. She takes her coat from the wardrobe. George sees a bright splash of blood on its back and realizes that it must have come from the top of the wardrobe. He puts his tortoise down and climbs on his desk to have a look. From the top of the wardrobe, he withdraws "his mis-fired arrow, on which is impaled Thumper." He hides his face in the fur, sobs, steps backwards, and . . . "CRRRRRUNCH! He has stepped, fatally, on Pat." It is a horrifying moment, and it brings the unspoken realization that George, in his clumsiness, is capable of having killed McFee accidentally and unknowingly.

George falls to the floor, and Act 2 ends on the sound of his sobs, which are amplified and repeated to bridge the transition into the play's short coda. The Coda is a bizarre, almost surrealistic presentation of the symposium on "Man—good, bad, or indifferent?," for which George has been preparing. George remains prone while Crouch, as Chairman, moniters "two minutes of approximate silence" in respect for McFee's memory, and then introduces Sir Archibald Jumper. Archie swings in on a rope, speaks a nonsensical mixture of philosophical and scientific jargon that is distorted to form such puns as "Darwin's origin of the specious," and receives sustained applause.

Captain Scott, the astronaut, is called. Archie speaks for him and glosses over the "goodness, badness, or indifference" of Scott's abandonment of his fellow astronaut on the moon. When George is offered a turn to question Scott, he rises and says, "Why should I cross-examine the figures of my dreams." Although it is thus thinly disguised as a dream sequence, the Coda actually presents Stoppard's own view of the chaotically disastrous consequences of too-rapid change in government. As he has said elsewhere, Stoppard does not believe in revolution, but in a gradual process of "growing enlightenment . . . the contagious values."[10]

The new Archbishop of Canterbury is called to the witness stand, but that former agnostic has—to Archie's consternation—begun to profess the beliefs that go with his charge. Archie's reaction is borrowed from two literary/historical sources. The first ("My Lord Archbishop, when I was last in Lambeth I saw good strawberries in your garden—I do beseech you send for some.") is a paraphrase of Richard's line to the Bishop of Ely in Shakespeare's *Richard III* (4.4):

> My Lord of Ely, when I was last in Holborn,
> I saw good strawberries in your garden there.
> I do beseech you send for some of them.

In Shakespeare's play the request is an evasive tactic, preparatory to Richard's condemnation of a former friend to death. Stoppard's second reference, "Will no one rid me of this turbulent priest!," recalls Henry II's indirect order that resulted in the murder, in 1170, of his former friend Thomas à Becket, whose appointment as Archbishop of Canterbury had led to a clash between church and state. This exclamation from Archie brings forth the jumpers in yellow gymnast's suits, who form a pyramid around Archbishop Clegthorpe. George apparently comprehends the situation, for he mutters about "proper respect for absolute values," but he makes no move to stop it.

There is a gunshot. Clegthorpe is blown out of the pyramid, which disintegrates. Dotty Moore is called. She sings her testimony—a song that includes the line "Show me where to stand, and I'll tell you my philosophy." Her relativistic views are interrupted by George's shout: "Stop!" George babbles quasi-coherently, until Archie interrupts him and, to end the play, placates our anxiety about modern life with an all-purpose panacea:

Do not despair—many are happy much of the time; more eat than starve, more are healthy than sick, more curable than dying; not so many dying as dead; and one of the thieves was saved. Hell's bells and all's well—half the world is at peace with itself, and so is the other half; vast areas are unpolluted; millions of children grow up without suffering deprivation, and millions, while deprived, grow up without suffering cruelties, and millions, while deprived and cruelly treated, none the less grow up. No laughter is sad and many tears are joyful. At the graveside the undertaker doffs his top hat and impregnates the prettiest mourner. Wham, bam, thank you, Sam.

Much of the success of *Jumpers* is due to the skill with which Stoppard exploits theatrical means to reify intellectual content. The play's very structure makes a comment: two acts of polemics-*cum*-murder-mystery in a realistic context are framed by the opening sequence and the coda, both of which are illogical and disorienting. The circularity of this structure (beginning and ending the play with the toppling of the gymnastic pyramid after a gunshot) recalls the work of some Absurdist playwrights like Ionesco, as critic John Weightman has pointed out. But Weightman also asked: "Why is the play weighted down at the end with the rather tedious coda? It could have stopped five minutes before it does. Is it because Mr Stoppard cannot quite control his flow of language and gimmicks?"[11] Despite Weightman's reservation, it seems obvious that the deliberate symmetry of the two surrealistic frame sequences is intended to confine George's metaphysical intellectualizing within the broader context of a world gone mad. The insanity of contemporary society is vividly evoked throughout the play by such devices as the television screen that brings the Rad-Lib election results and the aftermath of the moon-landing right into Dotty's bedroom, and the play's structure isolates a universe of imagination within that insanity.

Another theatrical value in *Jumpers* is the scenic metaphor. The two rooms in the setting, separated by a hallway, dichotomize the worlds of the academic and the artist. George's study is the domain of the intellect. In Dotty's bedroom, since she is an artist, the emotions predominate; it is also the realm of sensory experience, where games are played and meals are eaten. Complementing the sensory/emotional and the theoretical/ intellectual being is the pragmatic/physical side of any triangular construct of human responses. The latter is represented by Archie, who comes from the outside world; he is a man of action, whether it be in gymnastics or politics.

Scenic images—visual moments that make a statement and give a special vitality to the staging— abound in *Jumpers.* The gymnasts, who give the play its title, are the most striking example, closely seconded by the corpse that is so often moved from one spot in the bedroom to another, even hung on the back of the door. Other examples are the bow and arrows, the tortoise and the hare, the goldfish bowl, the television screen, the "very civilized lunch" on the tea trolley, the use of the spotlight on Dotty, the chandelier-swing and the rope-swing.

Stoppard's use of music as a theatrical device was rather tentative in *Rosencrantz and Guildenstern Are Dead*; it served to announce the coming of the tragedians. However, in *Jumpers,* Stoppard greatly strengthened that element of theatricality. Dotty's songs about the moon, the parade music on television, the recording of Dotty's singing that Bones brings and plays on her phonograph—all securely integrated with plot and character—serve to enhance the ideological or emotional focus of the scenes. In one cleverly conceived sequence, sound effects are juxtaposed with visual ones to create a kind of nonverbal pun: Dotty and Bones face each other in the softly lit bedroom, while romantic music is heard; Bones raises his head to speak, and we hear the trumpeting bray of an elephant; Bones drops his vase of flowers, and it sounds as if it is falling down a long flight of stone stairs. All of these sounds emanate coincidentally from George's tape recorder in the study, and they are repeated in the very different context of his subsequent discourse on the value of absolute aesthetic standards in distinguishing between music and noise.

George Moore, the bumbling protagonist of *Jumpers*, is the archetypal Stoppardian hero. Like George Riley in *Enter a Free Man*, Albert in *Albert's Bridge*, Moon in *Lord Malquist and Mr Moon*, and Henry Carr in *Travesties*, George is a man who functions at one remove from the center of events. He is never in control of, nor does he even fully understand the situation that his presence catalyzes. He is highly intelligent, but slighty out of touch with practical concerns. Most of these protagonists are dominated by women.

George Moore and Mr Moon both have reason to suspect their wives of infidelity, and both experience the same kind of despair, not so much at the probable transgression, as at the need to find explanations that contradict outward appearances. This irritates their desire for a sense of universal order, some kind of grand design in which they can place their confidence as they become hopelessly enmeshed in the chaos of day-to-day life in a technological society. This is, too, the satisfaction of bridge-painting in *Albert's Bridge:* getting free of the noise and chaos and looking down from a vantage point that makes society seem to fall into a safe pattern of dots and squares.

In its thematic concerns, as well as in patterns of characterization, *Jumpers* is a compendium of preoccu-

pations that emerge from the whole range of Stoppard's
writing. Paralleling the retreat from encroaching tech-
nology, in several other works as well as in *Jumpers*, is a
quest for style or for an aesthetic sensibility that could
make modern life tenable. The relationship of the artist
to society is frequently explored. Like Dotty, the artist
sometimes withdraws from society or is otherwise set
apart from its mainstream. The ending of *Jumpers* also
hints that the artist may be exploited, knowingly or not,
for political purposes. Awareness of death has remained
a constant factor, from *Rosencrantz and Guildenstern
Are Dead* to the plays that incorporate murder mys-
teries: *Jumpers*, *The Real Inspector Hound*, and *Artist
Descending A Staircase*. A race against time is often
implicit. Just as George works through the night to
prepare his symposium lecture, so are the journalists in
Night and Day pressured by a deadline to file their
stories.

Some of the most significant recurrent elements in
Jumpers and in numerous other works by Stoppard are
game-playing, confusion of names or identities, subtle
borrowings from Shakespeare, shifting perspectives on
the truth, and playful reversal of the audience's expectations. Of all Stoppard's works, the two that can be
most fruitfully compared with *Jumpers* are his novel,
Lord Malquist and Mr Moon, and his next full-length
play, *Travesties*.

The idea for *Travesties* was given to Stoppard years
before it began to coalesce into a play. A journalist
colleague in Bristol once mentioned to him that Russian revolutionary leader V.I. Lenin had lived in Zurich
during World War I at the same time as Tristan Tzara,
leader of the Dada revolution in art. One of Stoppard's
motives in basing the play on this historical coincidence
was the hope of answering, once and for all, his interviewers' questions about why he didn't write "political
plays." Stoppard has said that *Travesties* examines
"whether the words 'revolutionary' and 'artist' are capa-

ble of being synonymous, or whether they are mutually exclusive or something in between."[12] In the course of his research, he learned that James Joyce, whose *Ulysses* revolutionized the shape of the novel, had also lived in Zurich at that time. This gave him three "revolutionaries" with which to work. Richard Ellmann's biography, *James Joyce*, provided Stoppard with his fourth major character, Henry Carr, and with the literary peg on which to hang the play—*The Importance of Being Earnest* by Oscar Wilde.

In his preface to the published text of *Travesties*, Stoppard explains that James Joyce was the business manager of The English Players, a group composed of both professional and amateur English-speaking actors who were wartime residents of Zurich. For their first production, *The Importance of Being Earnest*, Joyce decided to cast in the role of Algernon a minor official he had noticed working in the British Consulate. This tall, good-looking young man, Henry Carr, had been wounded in the trenches, taken prisoner by the Germans, and sent as an exchange prisoner to Switzerland, where his path crossed that of James Joyce. Carr's performance in the play was enthusiastically received, but he and Joyce had a falling out when Joyce paid Carr only ten francs, the token amount agreed upon for amateur performers, instead of the thirty-franc fee paid to professionals.

In an ensuing court case, Carr claimed reimbursement for a pair of trousers he had bought to wear in the play, while Joyce demanded the money for five tickets that Carr had presumably sold. Joyce also sued for slander, since Carr had called him a "cad" and a "swindler." Joyce won on the money, but Carr won, with costs, on the slander.[13] It was in *Ulysses* that Joyce got his revenge, by conferring Carr's name upon a detestable minor character.

Having digested these facts, Stoppard began to

construct his flight of fancy for the stage. In an interview on *Travesties*, he described his creative process:

One's whole existence often comes out in a play. It consists of
unconscious collecting of possible material and the elimina-
tion of most of it. There's an element of fortune, coincidence,
and a sort of unconscious selection going on. There's enough
mystery in the process for me not to wish to disturb it too
much.[14]

There are examples in *Travesties* of that "element of
coincidence" that seems to work for playwrights. Stoppard tells how, after deciding to hinge his plot on that
of *The Importance of Being Earnest* and to make Tristan
Tzara's role in *Travesties* parallel that of Jack Worthing
in *Earnest* (a character who gives his own name to a
fictitious scapegrace brother), he discovered that "that
role was played in the Zurich production by an actor
whose first name was Tristan" (Tristan Rawson). Similarly, after deciding to use Joyce in the place of Lady
Augusta Bracknell (who is forbiddingly protective of
Gwendolen, the young lady Jack loves), Stoppard discovered that although Joyce was christened James Au-
gustine, it was erroneously recorded as James Augusta.
"But," says Stoppard, "I very seldom go into a play
thinking about that kind of fairly refined analytical
cross-reference structure. Obviously, the more material you have behind you, the greater the possibilities
are in arithmetical progression for cross-reference and
compass-point coordinates, as it were."[15] *Travesties*
was written in about ten months, from March 1972 to
January 1973. Stoppard recalled that he spent the first
five months "just worrying," but that from July to
January he wrote every day.[16]

    Travesties is a memory play. Like Tennessee
Williams's *The Glass Menagerie*, it presents a random
selection of moments from the past filtered through the
singular vision—and, perhaps, faulty memory—of a

character who moves in and out of the action he narrates. Stoppard chose Henry Carr as the character
whose recollections form the substance of the play, and
he conceived the role for actor John Wood, who had
played Guildenstern in *Rosencrantz and Guildenstern
Are Dead*. Stoppard has commented on Wood's ability
to move back and forth without benefit of makeup
changes, between the portrayal of Carr as an old codger
"huddled in his bathrobe . . . chainsmoking . . . wist-
fully scouring the lenses of his fogged-over memory"
and the young Carr whose main interests are sartorial
and who plays the drawing-room dandy Algernon to
perfection: "He has enough experience in his face to
cover the old man, plus he is physically and mentally
young enough to suggest youth and agility."[17]

Stoppard's decision to write what Charles
Marowitz has called a "play-within-a-monologue,"[18] instead of a historically accurate dramatization of events
in Zurich in 1917 and 1918, allowed him to mingle
"scenes which are self-evidently documentary . . . with
others which are just as evidently fantastical."[19] He
insists that he "did intend, throughout, a minor an-
thology of styles-of-play, styles-of-language. Some of it
is in rhyme; some of it is parody."[20] The result is "intellectual vaudeville."[21] *Newsweek* reviewer Jack
Kroll summed up the "dizzying collage of styles" and
its effect:

Joycean stream-of-consciousness, high comedy à la Oscar
Wilde, an antic scene spoken entirely in limericks, another
done to the tune of "Mr Gallagher and Mr Shean," still
another that parodies the great "catechism" chapter between
Stephen and Bloom in *Ulysses*. Technically all this works
because, as Stoppard says of himself, "I fall into comedy like a
man falling into bed." But underneath the mattress is a hard
board—Stoppard's lust for ideas.[22]

Historically, there is no evidence that Tristan
Tzara, James Joyce, and Vladimir Ilich Lenin ever met

while they lived in Zurich. Since none of them was then internationally renowned, it is quite possible that they all brushed shoulders in some public place without being aware of it. Stoppard chose the Zurich Public Library as the place where such an encounter is most likely to have occurred, and this is the setting in which the play opens. The Library setting also serves a symbolic function, representing the life of the mind, the realm of ideas, where fiction and fact exist side by side, just as Joyce and Lenin work there in physical, if not ideological, proximity. The other setting for the play is a room in the apartment of the nonintellectual Carr. Since Old Carr is supposed to have kept the same lodgings since the Great War, the Room reflects his closed and self-contained perspective.

The opening scene in the Library introduces the three "revolutionaries" and establishes—through a cacophony of tongues, with only sporadic phrases that are recognizably English—the international flavor of wartime Zurich. Tzara cuts up a page of writing word by word into his hat, shakes the hat, empties it onto the table, and reassembles the words into the following lines:

> Eel ate enormous appletzara
> key dairy chef's hat he'll learn oomparah!
> Ill raced alas whispers kill later nut east,
> noon avuncular ill day Clara!

These first lines of *Travesties* are a ready example of Stoppard's "facetiousness quotient," his deliberate use of jokes and references that will be picked up by almost nobody, but that stay in the play as "a small act of defiance" on his part and as "a bonus" for the happy few who catch them.[23] With some knowledge of French and with the published play text in hand, one might extract the following French words from Tzara's nonsense poem:

Il est énorme, s'appelle Tzara,
Qui déréchef se hâte. Hilare nonpareil!
Il reste à la Suisse parcequ'il est un artiste.
"Nous n'avons que l'art," il déclara![24]

These lines might also be interpreted as a parody of Lucky's long speech, in *Waiting for Godot*, which sounds very much like them. In any case, Tzara's recitation elicits an admonition from the librarian, Cecily.

At another table, James Joyce is dictating to a pretty young woman who we later learn is Carr's sister Gwen. For literary cognoscenti there is the bonus of recognizing lines from the Oxen in the Sun episode of *Ulysses:* "Deshilles holles eamus . . . ," "Hoopsa, boyaboy, hoopsa!" Joyce gives Gwen a folder, while Cecily crosses to Lenin to receive a similar folder from him. Without realizing it, the two women accidentally exchange folders.

Lenin's wife Nadya rushes in and tells him, in Russian, that the revolution has begun in St. Petersburg. Although no translation is provided, the meaning is clear when Lenin repeats the word "Revolutsia!" Lenin begins to gather up his papers, but drops one. Joyce picks it up, reads "U.S.A. 250 million marks, 28,000 workers . . . ," and returns it to Lenin with apologies in four languages. All of the characters exit, no significant encounter having taken place.

It becomes apparent that the entire vignette in the library was conjured up in the memory of the old man, Carr, who has been immobile on stage from the beginning. The scene shifts to Carr's Room, where the shambling, senile eccentric speaks a long, emotionally-colored monologue, reminiscing about his life and times as a friend of the famous. He begins with Joyce, whom he remembers as a limerick-spouting "Irish lout" from Dublin. He claims to have known Joyce well and to have recognized Joyce's genius at the height of his powers, when he was writing *Ulysses,* which "if memory serves" went under the working title "Elasticated Bloomers." Carr tries to appear magnanimous in his memorial portrait of Joyce, but the final brushstroke betrays his true feelings: "in short a liar and a hypocrite, a tight-fisted, sponging, fornicating drunk not worth the paper, that's that bit done."

Carr's memory jumps to Lenin, but now relies heavily upon abstractions and historical hindsight. He makes a great effort to remember what Lenin was really like, but all he can come up with is: "To those of us who knew him Lenin's greatness was never in doubt." Struck by the recollection that, if only he had bet a pound on Lenin's ultimate victory, he would be a millionaire today, Carr moves quickly on to his next subject, Tristan Tzara, who also lived in Spiegelgasses Street.

Actually Carr speaks less about Tzara than about the Dada movement in art that Tzara founded. "You remember Dada!—historical halfway house between Futurism and Surrealism . . . Dada!—down with reason, logic, causality, coherence, tradition, proportion, sense and consequence, my art belongs to Dada. . . ." Carr's meandering musings incorporate other literary puns that are still more recherché than this wordplay on Cole Porter's song "My Heart Belongs to Daddy."

A small sampling from Carr's monologue of these literate little jokes, some half-hidden, some obvious, will convey a sense of what critics refer to as Stoppard's "verbal fireworks" or "linguistic gymnastics." In the line quoted above, overshadowed by the more familiar song reference, there is, in "sense and consequence," a play on the title of Jane Austen's novel *Sense and Sensibility*. Carr refers to Joyce's celebrity after the publication of *Ulysses* as "caviar for the general public," thus ingeniously inverting the meaning of the line from Shakespeare's *Hamlet*: "The play, I remember, pleased not the million; 'twas caviare to the general." Ringing a change upon the Latin phrase *mutatis mutandis,* which means "with the necessary changes," Carr describes Zurich's "swiftly-gliding snot-green (mucus mutandis) Limmat River." Zurich is also characterized by "jewelled escapements and refugees of all kinds." An escapement is a moving part in a watch, the finest Swiss-made watches have jewels on these parts to prevent wear; the term also evokes the image of refugees escaping with only their jewels from war-ravaged Europe to neutral Switzerland.

Literary styles are parodied within Carr's monologue, as well as elsewhere in the play. Many epigrams sound as if they flowed directly from the pen of Oscar Wilde. In the passage on Lenin, Carr's use of rhythmic and sound values and his sentence construction (not to mention his mannered sprinkling of parentheses) are distinctly Nabokovian. His detailed directions for finding Lenin's house from the river, including descriptions of streets not taken, evoke Joyce's tours of Dublin in *Ulysses.* With reference to Lenin's apartment, he asks "who'd have thought big oaks from a corner room at number 14 Spiegelgasse?" (a pun on the proverb "big oaks from little *acorns* grow").

Carr then speaks of the Dadaists in Switzerland: "I well remember as if it were yesteryear (oh where are they now?) how Hugo Ball—or was it Hans Arp? yes!—no—Picabia, was it?—no, Tzara—yes!—wrote his name in the snow with a walking stick and said: There! I think I'll call it The Alps. Oh the yes-nos of yesteryear." And we subliminally hear the line "where are the snows of yesteryear?" from François Villon's "Ballade des dames du temps jadis." Alfred Lord Tennyson's "Charge of the Light Brigade" is the reference for Carr's rememberance of his own arrival in peaceful Switzerland from "howitzerland" during the Great War: "entente to the left, detente to the right,

into the valley of the invalided blundered and wandered myself when young."

Carr removes his dressing gown and appears as his
young self. His manservant Bennett carries in a tea-tray
with sandwiches, and their subsequent dialogue spoofs
the opening scene, between Algernon and his manservant, in *The Importance of Being Earnest*. Carr prattles
about the war and international affairs and about his
wardrobe, in the same breath, with equal concern. This
sequence contains several "time-slips," when Carr's
memory "jumps the rails" and has to be picked up again
with a repeated line. Thus, whenever the scene's progress bogs down in Carr's sartorial reminiscences or
other such distractions, Bennett recharges both the
memory and the scene, by saying, "I have put the
newspapers and telegrams on the sideboard, sir," to
which Carr replies, "Is there anything of interest?" By
this means, we are informed of the progress of the war
and of the unrest in Russia over a period of years at the
same time as the sequence moves gradually toward
Carr's meeting with Tristan Tzara, who had left his
calling card.

Oscar Wilde's graceful inversions of the accepted
order of things are echoed in the manner in which Carr,
a consular official, is kept informed of current events by
his manservant. So little does Carr grasp of the world
outside himself that his reaction to Bennett's announcement of a social revolution in Russia is: "A *social*
revolution? Unaccompanied women smoking at the
Opera, that sort of thing? . . ." And when Bennett explains that there have been scenes of violence between
the classes, Carr assumes that "the exploited class . . .
goaded beyond endurance by the insolent rapacity of
its servants" must have turned upon its butlers, foot-
men, cooks, and valets. Bennett tells Carr that "a betting man would lay odds of about a million to one

against Lenin's view prevailing," but at the same time he advises Carr to "put a pound on him."

Tristan Tzara arrives, followed immediately by James Joyce and Gwendolen. However, these are not the characters as we come to know them later in the play, but speeded-up nonsense versions. Tzara "has a French-Rumanian accent and he's monocled and outrageous."[25] Joyce is a caricature of a stage Irishman whose entrance speech, a limerick, initiates a sequence of dialogue among the four characters composed of twelve more limericks. The content of this short, manic scene is a barely intelligible version of Joyce's first meeting with Carr, which is staged again later in a more realistic style.

After a pause, Tzara arrives again, speaking correct English this time. In fact, Tzara and Carr behave like Jack Worthing and Algernon Moncrieff in *The Importance of Being Earnest,* but the substance of their long scene together is a discussion of the relationship of art and politics. Tzara's position is the same as that of the leftist writers of the 1960s and early 1970s, whose tactics Stoppard deplored. Tzara maintains, for example, that "doing the things by which is meant Art is no longer considered the proper concern of the artist. In fact it is frowned upon. Nowadays, an artist is someone who makes art mean the things he does. A man may be an artist by exhibiting his hindquarters. He may be a poet by drawing words out of a hat." Although Carr must be labeled a philistine, he marshals a good argument for distinguishing "between poetry and a sort of belle-litter," and rebuts Tzara with an expression of Stoppard's own point of view:

Wars are fought to make the world safe for artists. It is never quite put in those terms but it is a useful way of grasping what civilised ideals are all about. The easiest way of knowing whether good has triumphed over evil is to examine the freedom of the artist. The *ingratitude* of artists, indeed their hostility, not to mention the loss of nerve and failure of talent which accounts for "modern art," merely demonstrate the freedom of the artist to be ungrateful, hostile, self-centered and talentless, for which freedom I went to war, and a more selfless ideal for a man of my taste it would be difficult to imagine.

That ideal is "selfless" for Carr, a nonartist, because he believes that artists are members of a privileged class, that "to be an artist *at all* is like living in Switzerland during a world war," self-absorbed and exempt from the kind of responsibilities with which ordinary people—the majority of people—are burdened. Stoppard has expressed similar sentiments about himself as early as 1968 in an article published in the London *Sunday Times:*

I feel some guilt about being a writer. Probably all artists feel guilty. The reason is—at least this is how I analyse it for myself—that we are still lumbered with an enormous heritage of art, which has become something which folks place on the edge of society. Artists are made to feel decorators, embroiderers, who operate not precisely at the hub of society, who don't in fact contribute in the way that one can contribute a bicycle or a pound of butter, who somehow are in a business that can barely justify itself until we have enough butter and all that butter stands for.

It took me quite a long while to justify my own credentials; yet artists do not in fact need to justify themselves—they are producing something which crystallises and makes concrete something in the air.[26]

When the Tzara/Carr polemic reaches an impasse, there is a time-slip cue, and the two men start their scene once more from the beginning—this time to advance the action of the play instead of indulging in ideological debate. Paralleling the action of *The Importance of Being Earnest,* in which Jack Worthing visits Algernon in hopes of seeing Jack's cousin Gwendolen,

Tzara declares that he came to see Carr's sister Gwen
with the intention of proposing to her. Tzara complains
that he cannot get to speak to Gwendolen alone anywhere else, since she has apprenticed herself to James
Joyce. This is a surprise to Carr, who had supposed that
his sister's friend "Joyce" was a woman.

Carr says he will not consent to Gwendolen's mar-
rying a Rumanian, until Tzara explains "the whole
question of Jack." Carr had found Tzara's library card
which was made out to Jack Tzara. Just as in Oscar
Wilde's play, Worthing is "Ernest in town and Jack in
the country," so Tzara insists that his name is Tristan in
the Meierei Bar and Jack in the Library. Tzara explains
that the librarian, Cecily, is a disciple of Lenin, and
that Lenin—like most political revolutionaries—has
reactionary tastes in art. Lenin had wept to hear a
Beethoven sonata played on the bar piano, but had
lashed out against Dadaists after their "noise concert
for siren, rattle, and fire extinguisher." Thus, when
Tzara gave his last name in applying for a library card
and Cecily reacted unfavorably toward the reputation
of the Dadaist, Tzara told her that Tristan was his prod-
igal younger brother and that his own name was Jack.

Gwendolen arrives with James Joyce, and introduces him to Carr and Tzara. Joyce and Tzara know
each other by reputation and feel an instant antipathy.
"For your masterpiece," Tzara tells Joyce, "I have great
expectorations." Joyce turns to Carr with his proposal
that Carr play the leading role in the English Players'
production of *The Importance of Being Earnest*. Joyce
quickly assesses Carr's weakness and, when asked to
describe briefly the play's essentials, summarizes Act 1
like this: "The curtain rises. A flat in Mayfair. Teatime.
You enter in a bottle-green velvet smoking jacket with
black frogging—hose white, cravat perfect, boots
elastic-sided, trousers of your own choice."

Alone at last with Gwendolen, Tzara offers her his
latest poem: it is Shakespeare's eighteenth sonnet, cut

up into individual words and jumbled in a hat. He declares his love. Gwendolen reciprocates, adding that
she knew she was destined to love someone who shared
her regard for Mr Joyce as an artist. She gives Tzara the
folder she acquired in the opening scene, thus establishing that Tzara's respect for James Joyce (rather than
the name Ernest, as in *The Importance of Being
Earnest*) is a condition of her consent to marriage.

Joyce's reappearance breaks up their embrace. He
takes his hat and leaves by the main door. Gwendolen
exits to tell Carr of her marriage proposal. Then Joyce
reenters; he is covered with bits of paper—Tzara's
poem composed in Joyce's hat. "What is the meaning of
this?" he asks. Tzara replies: "It has no meaning. It is
without meaning as Nature is. It is Dada." This is followed by nearly seven pages of dialogue in which
Joyce quizzes Tzara, in the hair-splitting style of the
"Ithaca" catechism in *Ulysses*, about the development
of Dada. It is a passage that seems more strikingly out
of context than do the other stylistically distinctive sequences in *Travesties*, and yet Stoppard has expressed
particular satisfaction with it:

It exists almost on three levels. On one it's Lady Bracknell
quizzing Jack. Secondly, the whole thing is actually structured on [the eighth] chapter in *Ulysses*, and thirdly it's telling the audience what Dada is, and where it comes from.[27]

Kenneth Tynan has remarked that this "layer cake of
pastiche" exemplifies the essential problem of the play
as a whole: its lack of narrative thrust—to impel the
characters toward a credible state of crisis, anxiety, or
desperation. The scene, according to Tynan, "resem-
bles a triple-decker bus that isn't going anywhere."

From a dramaturgical standpoint, Tynan's comment cannot be disputed. The sequence is completely
static, and the play's forward impetus, even with the
underlying machinery of *The Importance of Being Earnest*, is minimal. But, theatrically, the sequence and

the play hold the audience's interest, because Stoppard
finds so many ways to distract attention from his structural failings. What *Travesties* lacks in plot and character is compensated for by sparkling dialogue, hearty
humor, lightweight brainteasers and serious idea content. There is also some exceptionally well-conceived
stage business.

The scene between Tzara and Joyce culminates in
stage business that, besides its pure entertainment
value, serves as objective correlative to the thought.
Joyce becomes a magician pulling tricks out of his hat.
The bits of paper he picks off his hair and clothes are
put back into his hat, from which he withdraws a carna-
tion that is apparently made of the same paper. The
metaphor is clear: whereas Tzara's "art" is to cut to
pieces the works of earlier artists, Joyce conjures new
wonders. From the same hat, Joyce also pulls out silk
handkerchiefs and flags. In his final speech, Joyce
squelches Tzara, telling him that "an artist is the magician put among men to gratify—capriciously—their
urge for immortality" and explaining how his *Ulysses*
will do this. He pulls a rabbit from the hat and exits.

Old Carr ends Act 1 of *Travesties* with another
rambling reminiscence. He recounts the court cases he
and Joyce brought against each other. Although he regarded the verdict as "a travesty of justice," Carr tried
to fantasize his revenge. He dreamed that he cross-
examined Joyce in the witness box and got him to admit
he was wrong, but then made the mistake of asking:
"And what did you do in the Great War?" "I wrote
Ulysses," Joyce responded. "What did you do?"

When the audience comes back from intermission,
Cecily is already on stage, waiting patiently until
everyone is seated. Then she begins to lecture on the
history of Marxist-Leninist thought. It is a rather dry,
factual lecture, until she brings it up to date, that is, to
1917. The lights come up on the Library set, where
Lenin and Joyce are seen at their work. She breaks off

when Carr enters, very debonair in his blazer, cream flannels and boater. His manner betrays the fact that he has come to spy on Lenin. He hands Cecily Tzara's visiting card, and she recognizes the name as that of "Jack's decadent nihilist younger brother." Carr is thus forced into a role that is the very opposite of his own personality.

In a long scene punctuated by several "time-slip" cues, Carr leads Cecily on to brag of her association with Lenin and to reveal what she knows. Carr learns that the Marxists have intercepted telegrams addressed to him as British Consul, but that they could not interpret such cryptic messages as "Break a leg" and "Drive 'em Wilde." Without revealing his own identity, he tells Cecily that the apparent flurry of activity at the Consulate was due to the Consul's part in The English Players' production. Cecily replies: "That would no doubt explain why he virtually left the Consulate's affairs in the hands of his manservant—who, fortunately, has radical sympathies." Carr thus learns that his servant Bennett has been passing British diplomatic secrets to Tzara.

Their conversation turns into an argument over the social utility of art, which Cecily affirms and Carr denies. Despite their disagreement, Carr is charmed by Cecily and offers to let her reform him. She gives him the folder she had received in the opening scene, telling him that it contains an article by Lenin that advocates more stringent socialist principles in Western European governmental policy. This leads into a polemic on the practical application of Marxist principles. Cecily finally accuses Carr of being a "patronising Kant-struck prig" who, even as he talks about social classes, is trying to imagine how she would look stripped to her knickers.

The scene briefly moves one step farther from reality. Filtered first through Carr's memory, reality is additionally distorted when we see what he was imagining about her. While she continues the conversation on political theory, Cecily climbs onto the library desk. Colored lights play over her body, and a big-band rendition of "The Stripper" accompanies her incantatory speech composed of socialist cant phrases. There is another time-slip, and the lights snap back to normal. Cecily and Carr declare their mutual love. The end of their scene together touches bases with *The Importance of Being Earnest,* as well as providing a moment of visual comedy in the style of bedroom farce:

CECILY: Ever since Jack told me he had a younger brother who was a decadent nihilist it has been my girlish dream to reform you and to love you.

CARR: Oh, Cecily!

(*Her embrace drags him down out of sight behind her desk. He re-surfaces momentarily—*)

But, my dear Cecily, you don't mean that you couldn't love me if—

(*—and is dragged down again.*)

Lenin's wife Nadya enters and, baldly addressing the audience, narrates Lenin's activities from the moment he received news of the revolution in Russia to his departure by train from Zurich. While Lenin hovers on stage like a lecturer's visual aid, she quotes from his letters and telegrams, and recounts his elaborate plans for traveling back to Russia in disguise. This history lesson does not bore the audience, because it is interspersed with zany glimpses of Carr, Tzara, and Cecily. At one point, when Tzara learns that Carr has passed himself off as a younger, scapegrace Tzara and Cecily runs off weeping over her failure to make peace between the two "brothers," Lenin shows his disgust, by removing the wig disguise in which he planned to travel through Germany and turning away from them. His understated gesture points up the antithesis between Lenin's grandiose schemes to change the course of civilization and the supercivilized veneer of Oscar Wilde.

Old Carr interrupts Nadya's discourse with an apology for not having "stopped the whole Bolshevik thing in its tracks" when he had the chance. He failed to act because of uncertainty about the right thing to do and because of his feelings for Cecily. He recalls, too, that "*he wasn't Lenin then! I* mean *who was he*? as it were." By the time Carr was ready to act decisively, Lenin had gone. Only in a later scene do we learn that Carr was ordered in a telegram from the minister to prevent at all costs Lenin's leaving Switzerland.

Stoppard suggests the use of a projection screen to show photographs of Lenin's triumphal return to Russia. Lenin and Nadya continue, however, to speak to the audience, offering extensive documentation of Lenin's attitudes toward art. It is essential to Stoppard's purpose that Lenin's views be revealed in counterpoint to all that Tzara, Joyce, and Carr have said. (The man who presided over history's greatest social upheaval actually respected traditional values in art; he was suspicious of modern art, which he could neither understand nor enjoy.) But the drawback to the placement of this densely written five-page sequence so near the end of the play is its nondramatic quality. It is purely informative, as if Stoppard could not restrain himself from sharing all the fascinating gleanings of his historical research. The character study of Lenin is interesting but gratuitous; it exists apart from the dramatic action of the play. The limitations of the sequence are finally transcended in Lenin's last speech, which refers to Beethoven's "Appassionata" Sonata:

. . . I can't listen to music often. It affects my nerves, makes me want to say nice stupid things and pat the heads of the people who while living in this vile hell can create such beauty. Nowadays we can't pat heads or we'll get our hands bitten off. We've got to *hit* heads, hit them without mercy, though ideally we're against doing violence to people. . . .

This single speech sums up, more clearly than do all the preceding pages on Lenin's aesthetic sensibilities, the ruthlessness of the man's politics and the universally affective power of art.

Lenin and Nadya leave. The "Appassionata" gives way to "Mr Gallagher and Mr Shean," a music-hall patter sequence performed by Gwendolen and Cecily as a skillful parody of the tea-table dialogue in *The Importance of Being Earnest*. In this case, Gwendolen and Cecily discover that they are both engaged to a man named Tristan Tzara. Apparently, the real Tristan Tzara, in order to please Gwendolen, has professed to espouse art for art's sake, while Henry Carr, known and loved by Cecily as Tristan Tzara, has come to understand the social utility of art.

The misunderstanding is resolved when Tzara and Carr enter, each carrying the folder that was lent to him. Asked for their opinions, both men admit to having disliked what they read. Allan Rodway has pointed out the travesty inherent in their responses: "The communist Tzara thinks Lenin's writing worthless when he believes it to be Joyce's, while Carr, the aesthete, thinks Joyce's writing rubbish when he believes it to be by Lenin."[28] The two women feel obliged to break off their engagements.

Joyce enters and haggles with Carr over the missing theater tickets and the trousers Carr bought for the play. Tzara joins the fray, handing Joyce the folder he had read and condemning its lack of "charm or even vulgarity." Joyce then assumes his Lady Bracknell function in the play and discovers (instead of the parentage of a handbag as in Wilde's play) that the folder contains not a chapter of *Ulysses* but a socialist tract. Carr then realizes that he had read Joyce's work instead of Lenin's. The revelation that Tzara and Carr had disliked their reading only because they had both read from the wrong folders justifies Gwendolen's and Cecily's reconciliation with them. There is a "rapid but formal climax, with appropriate cries of 'Cecily! Gwendolen! Henry! Tristan!' and appropriate embraces"—a travesty of the well-made play's ending.

A ritual dance of the couples provides a transition into the brief postscript. Carr and Cecily dance out of view to return as Old Carr and Old Cecily. The eighty-year-old Cecily begins to correct her husband's memories. His chronology was all wrong: Lenin left Zurich in 1917, and *The Importance of Being Earnest* was not produced there until 1918. Carr never even saw Lenin, only visited cafés that Lenin had once frequented. Carr was not the British Consul, but only a minor official; the Consul's name was Bennett. These corrections bring the sudden realization that Carr's memories were all quite false and that the entire evening's exercise was a travesty.

Like the play itself, the title *Travesties* operates on several levels of meaning. Besides the obvious travesties of *Ulysses* and *The Importance of Being Earnest*, there are the numerous smaller-scaled pastiches of literary styles and of various modes of entertainment, ranging from the burlesque strip show to the platform lecture. Reviewers have interpreted the title as Stoppard's admission of his own impertinence in borrowing from so many sources, as a comment on what occurs when memory is ravaged by time, and as the license that is taken with historical probability. According to Allan Rodway, "*Travesties* travesties both the literature and the lives it is based on, in the cause of something other than 'the facts.' Concerned *with* the problem of knowledge, however, it is unconcerned *about* it."[29] Whereas Pinter and Beckett distort reality by withholding information, Stoppard has been accused of blurring the edge between illusion and reality by providing an excess of information, mostly in elliptical form. Excess there may be; but deliberate falsification there is not. One must not infer, Stoppard insists, that because *Travesties* does not present "real" events in Zurich in 1917, he does not believe in real, truthful history. His rationale, which may be construed from the play itself, is stated succinctly elsewhere: intellectually, he subscribes "to objective truth and to absolute morality. . . . But art is not the child of pure intellect, it is equally the child of temperament. That is why it is art. And most of all, that is why it must be distinguished from other human pursuits which can indeed be true or false."[30]

Given this orientation, one may indeed wonder why Stoppard did not choose to write a stylized version of Lenin, to blend in with the rest of the play. Stoppard's serious treatment of Lenin has been the single major stumbling block in just about every critical appreciation of *Travesties*. Since Lenin and his wife Nadya are the only characters not distorted by Carr's self-serving memory, the audience's acceptance of the flashback convention is jarred. On the other hand, it has been argued that a historical figure of such massive proportions as Lenin is too firmly rooted in reality for acceptance on a level of fantasy.

In response to the suggestion that Lenin and Nadya might have been given the roles of Oscar Wilde's Reverend Chasuble and Miss Prism, Stoppard said "that would have killed the play because of trivialization." Whereas most critics felt that Lenin's long monologue (according to Kenneth Tynan, "a weighty cargo," under which the whole play "slowly capsizes and sinks"[31]) interrupts the fun and "makes it a bit difficult to get back into the party-going mood of the rest of the play,"[32] Stoppard has defended it: "I believe that that section saves *Travesties* because I think one's just about *had* that particular Wilde joke at that point. I wanted the play to stop—to give the audience documentary illustration of what Lenin felt about art and so on, and then carry on with the play."[33]

Interestingly, Stoppard justifies the sequence on a structural basis:

What I was trying was this. What I'm always trying to say is "Firstly, A. Secondly, minus A." What was supposed to be happening was that we have this rather frivolous nonsense going on, and then the Lenin section comes in and says, "Life is too important. We can't afford the luxury of this artificial frivolity, this nonsense going on in the arts." Then he says, "Right. That's what I've got to say," and he sits down. Then the play stands up and says, "You thought *that* was frivolous? You ain't seen nothin' yet." And you go into the Gallagher and Shean routine. That was the architectural thing I was after.[34]

It is, in fact, a dramaturgical experiment that fails the acid test of audience response.

A more elemental explanation of the documentary approach to Lenin might be that it enables the audience to perceive just how contradictory, viciously calculating, and even petty, the man and his ideas were. The ideological point is thus made without manipulation by the playwright. Substantively, Lenin convicts himself, and, emotionally, he loses favor with the audience by boring it. Again, however, what works in theory is altered by performance. When the actor and actress playing Lenin and Nadya walk out on stage, according to Stoppard, they are so human "you don't really think that man has contradicted himself throughout and condemned himself out of his own mouth. You think he really had a burden to carry, and Ashkenazy is doing his bit in the loudspeaker, playing the Appassionata. The equation is different, and even I am seduced by it."[35]

The handling of Lenin remains a minor but obvious fault in an otherwise artistically solid play. Presumably this was a problem Stoppard had in mind when he said that there were things he would like to change if it were not too late, but the play is dead to him now. "Most of *Travesties*—not as a structure and a play but speech by speech—still seems to me as good as I can ever get. It's slightly worrying actually. A lot of things in *Travesties* and *Jumpers* seem to me to be the terminus of the particular kind of writing which I can do."[36]

According to Stoppard, *Jumpers* and *Travesties* are so similar that a third variation on the pattern would be a bore. His view of their resemblance is largely in terms of structure:

You start with a prologue which is slightly strange. Then you have an interminable monologue which is rather funny. Then you have scenes. Then you end up with another monologue. And you have unexpected bits of music and drama, and at the same time people are playing ping-pong with various intellectual arguments.[37]

One might add that in the hands of any other playwright the murder mystery in *Jumpers* or the mix-up of folders in *Travesties* would provide more impetus for the plot. For Stoppard, however, these are almost incidental devices, to be picked up or dropped at random when there is a lull in the ping-pong dialectic.

Jumpers and *Travesties* have similar stage settings. George's study and the Zurich Public Library tend to be sacrosanct areas reserved for the characters with active intellectual lives; all others are intruders. Dotty's bedroom and Carr's room both serve, despite the neuroses or eccentricity of their principle occupant, as thoroughfares for the traffic of everyday life—dressing, dining, playing games, receiving visitors.

There are strong parallels between George Moore and Henry Carr, and between Dotty and Cecily. George and Carr are both ineffectual men. They have all the right instincts, but cannot get themselves taken seriously. Dotty and Cecily are women of charm and intelligence who have hobnobbed with great men of ideas (Dotty with Bertrand Russell, Cecily with V.I. Lenin), but who marry insignificant men. Both have had careers—Dotty as a singer, Cecily as a librarian. Both are led astray by leftist thought, but ultimately remain supportive of their husbands. Both disrobe seductively on stage, but manage to keep their aura of innocence.

Another similarity of characterization—or, at least, of dramatic function—may be seen in Sir Archibald Jumper and James Joyce, for they are the ones pulling the strings of the action. Jumper disposes of McFee's new ideas as well as of his corpse, diagnoses Dotty, gets rid of Bones, and holds the power to promote George to the Chair of Logic. Joyce handles the casting for The English Players, one-ups both Tzara and Carr in discussion, and writes *Ulysses*. Besides Lenin, they are the two characters with the greatest sense of their own identities.

Identity is one of Stoppard's recurring preoccupations. It surfaces in *Jumpers* and *Travesties*, as well as in many of his other works, most noticeably when one character cannot remember another's name and uses a succession of wrong ones. In *Jumpers*, Bones refers to George as Charlie, Jack, Ferdinand, Sidney, Clarence, and Wilfred, and to Archie Jumper as Sir Jim and Sigmund. In *Travesties*, Carr gets stuck on the idea that Joyce is a girl's name and uses Doris, Janice, Phyllis, and Deirdre on James Joyce.

Other points of comparison in *Jumpers* and *Travesties* are common to much of Stoppard's writing. Momentous events often serve as backdrop to the action—like the Rad-Lib election victory and the British moon-landing in *Jumpers,* and the Great War raging all around Switzerland in *Travesties.* Within the action, there is always some significant reversal of expectations, and yet the situation at the end is pretty much what it was at the beginning—the characters do not learn or change through experience. The confrontations between moral and pragmatic philosophy in *Jumpers,* and between art and politics in *Travesties,* may be subsumed by the larger question of the relativity of truth. Stoppard's willingness to examine and to deploy on stage complex notions about philosophy, history, politics, and art is also characteristic, as is the resulting potpourri of cosmic vision and trivia.

The special brilliance of both *Jumpers* and *Travesties* is their skillful integration of form and content. These two plays are even more theatrical than *Rosencrantz and Guildenstern Are Dead,* and *Jumpers* is probably Stoppard's masterpiece. Besides its imaginative use of stage images to animate philosophical thought, the play operates on a subtly zany level of reality and makes it credible. Its thoroughgoing intellectualism is supported on an emotional undercurrent that occasionally wells up to the surface. *Jumpers* is the most conceptually original and technically daring of Stoppard's plays.

4

Narrative Prose on the Sidelines: Short Stories and a Novel

"You mean I've been speaking prose for more than forty years without knowing it?," Monsieur Jourdain exclaims to his Philosophy Master in Molière's comedy, *Le Bourgeois Gentilhomme*. Insecurely seeking a mentor to teach him to write, like Molière's would-be gentleman of 300 years ago, Tom Stoppard emulated various masters, without realizing that he always had a style of his own. The basic elements of that style can be detected in his early published fiction, which is prose not written for the stage.

So closely is Stoppard's name linked with British theatre of the 1970s, one almost forgets that he has been a journalist, a short story writer, and a novelist. He still writes newspaper articles upon occasion, but he has abandoned the novel and the short story since 1966. He will undoubtedly follow through on a recent invitation to write a children's book, and this possibly will lead to new experiments in narrative prose. However, the works discussed in this chapter were all written before his first success as a playwright.

Stoppard's three short stories, "Reunion," "Life, Times: Fragments," and "The Story," were written in 1963. Their publication in *Introduction 2: Stories by New Writers* (London: Faber and Faber, 1964) saved this characteristic sampling from oblivion. Stoppard's now-familiar flair for words, as well as his gift for understatement, may be detected in them, but there is also an uncharacteristic personal element that he later found embarrassing and that he was able for the most part to overcome in the novel, *Lord Malquist and Mr Moon*, published in 1966. One common thread in these works is the awareness of passing time. Time is measured in "Reunion" by a silence that ebbs and flows like the sea; in "Life, Time: Fragments" by the age of the central character, given in each paragraph; in "The Story" by a documentary-style chronology of events; and in *Lord Malquist and Mr Moon* by the hours ticking away on the bomb that Moon carries about with him. This was the period in Stoppard's life when he was conscious of growing older faster than he was achieving the literary reputation to which he aspired. Derivative and unformed as they are, Stoppard's early efforts in narrative prose suggest that a substantial novelistic talent may be dormant and awaiting a reawakening stimulus.

Several influences are apparent in "Reunion," among them a Joycelike intoxication with words and Ronald Firbank's intellectual aestheticism. The choice of subject—a man's detached and depersonalized interaction with a woman in an unromantic setting—recalls aspects of T.S. Eliot's *Prufrock* and "The Hollow Men." The emphasis on capturing a fleeting state of mind even more explicitly than the external events that trigger it recalls Nathalie Sarraute's tropisms. In fact, Sarraute's own definition of "tropisms" provides a context for interpreting Stoppard's short story:

They are undefinable movements which glide very rapidly to the limit of consciousness; they are at the root of our gestures, our words, of the feelings we manifest, which we believe we feel and which we can define. They seemed to me and still seem to me to constitute the secret source of our existence. When these movements are in the process of formation, they remain unexpressed—not one word emerges—not even in the words of an interior monologue; they develop within us and vanish with extreme rapidity, without our ever really perceiving them clearly; they produce within us frequently very intense, but brief, sensations; these can be communicated to the reader only through images, thereby giving them an equivalent and enabling them to feel analogous situations. These movements had to be decomposed and allowed to extend into the reader's conscious mind in the manner of a film in slow motion. Time was no longer experienced in terms of the workaday world, but rather in a distorted and aggrandized present.[1]

The first sentences of "Reunion" seem tailormade to illustrate the concept of the tropism:

He counted to himself without thinking the words of any figure to stop at, just keeping deliberate track of the silence. He couldn't stop it coming. It kept coming like the sea, never falling back as far as it came, and each time it came close he started counting till it went away, and then it went away and he was still there, untouched, careful.

There is a snatch of awkward, disembodied conversation—words that have nothing to do with the interior movement, serving only to suggest an anecdote to which the tropisms are tied.

The anecdotal elements are simple: the man sits at a woman's kitchen table, as if interviewing her. He had come unannounced, and she had not fixed herself up. They had once had an affair, and he, whether momentarily under her spell again or merely feeling sorry for himself, would like to resume it. He would also like to prolong the present moment despite the expected arrival of her husband, a "dashing artistic type."

He contemplates picking up the bottle of milk from the table and smashing it on the sink; maybe this "spilt milk" gesture would define the situation and allow him to regain his equilibrium. Instead, he stalls, by talking of his obsession with a certain word "which if shouted at the right pitch and in a silence worthy of it, would nudge the universe into gear. You understand me, it would have to be shouted in some public place like the British Museum. . . . And that's not all. I'm almost sure that to know what the word is in advance would muck the whole thing up. It must be stumbled upon loudly and spontaneously, in exactly the right circumstances. It will probably turn out to be an obscenity." Or it might be an embarrassing word like "Love." Or a word in another language: "pafflid, brilge, culp, matrap, drinnop, guelp, trid, crik, christ."

The unknown word is, of course, a metaphor for whatever action, gesture, revelation, mindset, or fortuitous circumstances causes a person to find himself and get his life in balance. Stoppard became lyrical, or personal, or both, at the prospect: "His world will have shuddered into a great and marvellous calm in which books will be written and flowers picked and loves contemplated."

The man changes his tactics. He begins to talk about her: "What I miss is you approaching down busy streets . . . and watching you being pleased and watching you sitting in a chair . . . ," but what obsesses him most is "you in bed." Her simple "yes" response might be her consent to lovemaking or merely a disinterested acknowledgement of her presence in the conversation. It scarcely matters, for the story's final lines of dialogue, which allow either interpretation, culminate in an equally ambiguous ending. The man experiences some kind of intense frustration—sexual, emotional, or possibly even spiritual—and then a letdown:

"Oh, shut up," the woman said, finally, and the hollow ballooned, shaking emptily, his body disconnecting and the sea coming up fast, beyond relief from ritual counting or public obscenities, where only murder would stop it now, and it

took a long time, stairs and streets later, before he got a hold
on it again, without, as always, having murdered anybody.

The man in Stoppard's story is truly one of T.S. Eliot's
"hollow men":

> Between the idea
> And the reality
> Between the motion
> And the act
> Falls the Shadow

Just as "the word" eludes the man in "Reunion," so is it
missing in "The Hollow Men":

> For Thine is
> Life is
> For Thine is the
>
> *This is the way the world ends*
> *This is the way the world ends*
> *This is the way the world ends*
> *Not with a bang but a whimper.*

A purely anecdotal reading of "Reunion" like Ronald
Hayman's—which sees it as the story of a
seduction[2]—misses the "slow motion" plumbing of the
mind of a man given over to despair. And yet, the
double entendres in the story are certainly intentional.
"Reunion" is early evidence of Stoppard's skill at giving
comic overtones to a serious subject.

  "Life, Times: Fragments" is a brief, disjointed account of the works and days of a would-be writer whose
reputation is made only after the discovery of his
suicide by a self-serving literary critic. It raises the
philosophical question of whether a writer's work can
be separated from his life. We are given one-paragraph
glimpses of the writer at his first job, at ages 25, 27, 34,
50, and just before his death. He becomes—after his
professional loss of innocence in the first two anecdotes
and the moral compromise he makes at the age of

27—increasingly petty and unsympathetic. The limitations within himself suggest the limits of the man's ability to write. Only one paragraph is written in the present tense, when the fifty-year-old writer mentions having begun cataloguing his despair. All the earlier paragraphs were apparently written from this perspective. The following paragraph, which describes the writer just before his death, might then be the contribution of the critic, and it is a still further detached observer who tells us, in the last paragraph, that "the most famous critic in the land" has fabricated the writer's posthumous reputation out of the sensational fact of his death.

Another interpretation of the story is suggested by its use of the shifting point of view. Since the paragraphs alternate between first- and third-person narration, the third-person anecdotes (including the reporting of the suicide and the critic's exploitation of it) may be interpreted as samples of the first-person narrator's writing. In this case, the writer does not actually kill himself, but only creates a fictional suicide, and his comments about the critic lend a touch of Nabokovian irony. Again, since there is no change in tone, style, or characterization, we see that it is impossible to distinguish between the artist and his art.

There is also an element of autobiography in "Life, Times: Fragments." In the opening paragraph, the storyteller recounts a devastating mistake he made as a beginning reporter. The actual incident may or may not have happened to Stoppard during his newspaper days in Bristol, but the man's initial naiveté, his private agony, and, finally, his self-mockery sound much like Stoppard himself. The second anecdote, told in the third person, about a twenty-five-year-old reporter from the provinces who goes to London, is based upon Stoppard's personal experience. Interviewed for a job by the editor of the *Evening Standard,* the writer professes an interest in politics, but then must admit that he cannot name the Foreign Secretary. Afterwards, he consoles himself that it was a lucky escape from entrapment in a narrow journalistic job: "I'll have a shot at a novel, he thought. Then I can make the Foreign Secretary anybody I bloody well like."

Stoppard was twenty-six when he wrote this story, but in the third paragraph he may have been thinking of the turn his own life had taken three years earlier while vacationing on Capri. In the story he says:

I was twenty-seven then, exactly, and that was the beginning of something else. I was sitting up to my navel in sea when I remembered I was not twenty-six any more, and whatever it was I'd been waiting for slipped by then, between waves, as quickly as that. I was twenty-six and biding my time and when the next wave came I was twenty-seven and losing.

The writer in the story then allows himself to be kept by a rich woman: she is a metaphor for the security of a creativity-sapping job that Stoppard himself rejected when he quit journalism to gamble on becoming a serious writer. The remainder of "Life, Times: Fragments" can thus be seen as a projection into the future of the road not taken by Stoppard.

The writer in the story never moves beyond newspaper writing, except in his fantasies. In "the thirty-fourth year of his obscurity," he disdainfully dismisses the accepted literary models: Balzac, Flaubert, Stendhal, Wilde, Thackeray, Tolstoy, Turgenev, Proust, Lawrence, Kafka, Hemingway. He declares to his mistress that he will do it on his own: "I am—I feel—seminal!" But she offers no outlet for these creative urges. At fifty, as "the oldest sub in London," even those energies have been dissipated. He is thoroughly compromised: "Give us this day our daily press, and forgive us our intrusions into private grief. . . . Lead us into sensation and deliver us from libel. . . ." In the last glimpse of the man in his lifetime, he goes so far as

to pray for forgiveness for ever having aspired to being
a writer. Even the Lord responds with the rejection-
slip formula. Having made fun of his journalistic begin-
nings, Stoppard then used the ending for a gentle jab at
critics, to whose number he had also belonged.

"The Story" also draws upon Stoppard's familiarity
with behind-the-scenes operations in the newspaper
business. It is about a news story that gets blown up out
of proportion and causes a suicide. "The Story" is told
in a straightforward manner, in simple declarative sentences, by the reporter on whose conscience it weighs.
The incident occurred "a couple of years ago," but the
guilt feelings have just resurfaced as a result of a chance
encounter.

The reporter had spent a full day at an out-of-town
law court, and nothing noteworthy had turned up.
There was a minor case in which a schoolmaster from
another town was fined twenty-five pounds for inde-
cently touching a little girl he was teaching to swim,
but the reporter decided not to bother with it and even
mentioned to the man as he was leaving that it would
not be used. But, back in town, he ran into an old
friend from the Press Services, who urged him to
phone it in to Press Services—an arrangement by
which a reporter salaried by a newspaper would be paid
extra. The filing of that three-paragraph story with that
service led to his being pressured for more details by a
tabloid and by the schoolmaster's hometown daily, and
then the reporter had to cover himself with his own
paper by expanding the story still further. A week later
the schoolmaster was in the papers again, after he
threw himself in front of a subway train.

The reporter's insistence that he had finally got the
incident out of his mind is belied by his specific recall
of dates, names, and even the amount he earned from
the news item: "That made £3 2s. 6d. I don't know
what I spent it on. It got mixed up with my other

money and at the end of the month I was broke as usual." The unembellished, matter-of-fact style leaves the reader to his own conclusions. According to Ronald Hayman, it is clear that Stoppard "shares the guilty feeling that in living by telling tales on other individuals, the reporter is often destructive and sometimes murderous."[3] The question of the morality of a free press is taken up again in Stoppard's 1978 play *Night and Day*. "The Story," unpretentious as it is, provides Stoppard's canon with a paradigm of the traditional short story.

Stoppard's only novel, *Lord Malquist and Mr Moon*, is quite different from "The Story," and it is more typical of his work. The reader responds to technique more than to content, to a brilliance that is largely on the surface. The rationale of the novel might be summed up in the words of the two central characters. According to Lord Malquist, "substance is ephemeral, but style is eternal." The other main character, the intellectual leap-frogger Moon, says, "How can one be consistent about anything, since all the absolutes discredit each other?"

Consistency of style is deliberately violated in the first chapter, "Dramatis Personae and Other Coincidences," which composed of a number of successive pastiches that introduce five discrete groups of characters. In the first, and longest, section, we meet the title characters as they jounce through the streets of London in Lord Malquist's coach, drawn by a pair of pigeon-colored horses. Moon records Lord Malquist's thoughts in a notebook, but, somehow, as he jots them down, a concept like "cosmic accuracy" becomes "comic inaccuracy."

The lilac-gloved Lord Malquist expounds the idea that the history of the world viewed from the proper distance is nothing; that, considered on a grand scale, the world has not changed at all despite revolutions and technological innovations. Moon's contrasting view is stated in a later scene, when he tells of his attempt to write a history of the world. The task became insurmountable when "he experienced a vision of the billion interconnecting moments that lay behind and led to his simplest action, a vision of himself straightening his tie as the culminating act of a sequence that fled back into pre-history and began with the shift of a glacier."

In the coach Moon has difficulty concentrating on his Boswellian task. He lapses into mental interviews with himself, and he puts his hand in his pocket to feel the bomb he is carrying there. Turning a corner, the coach runs down a fat woman who seemed to be thrusting a petition at them. Lord Malquist flings back a handful of gold coins, but does not stop the coach. The coins turn out to be foil-wrapped chocolates, and the image of the unfurling roll of white paper, used several times in the novel, later resolves itself not as a petition but as toilet paper. The woman, however, is dead. This entire passage is written in a meticulous and understated tone reminiscent of Vladimir Nabokov.

The next section, in the style of Western pulp fiction, sets up a rivalry between two cowboys, Long John Slaughter and Jasper Jones. There is manic humor in the way L.J. repeatedly says, "Whoa, boy," to what the narrative equally often refers to as a mare. It is hinted much later that the cowboys are actors in a commercial for canned western-style pork and beans.

Another very brief section describes a white woman staggering with thirst and fatigue while, ten yards away, from behind a scrub of thorn, a lion watches her. Only later do we learn that the woman is Lord Malquist's wife and that the scene, which evokes an African-bush adventure, actually occurs in Green Park, where she had found their runaway pet lion Rollo. In a separate scene, a dark, barefoot man in a linen robe, who speaks with an Irish brogue and later identifies himself as the Risen Christ, rides a donkey into the heart of the city.

The narrative tone shifts to one of Regency romance, in a section that lyrically describes the lovely but proud Jane awaiting her beau. It will eventually become clear that Jane is Moon's wife and that her visitor is the cowboy Jasper Jones. In the course of the novel, Jane is seen in compromising situations with a succession of suitors, most notably with Lord Malquist, while she continues to project an air of sweetness and innocence. Suspicious of appearances, as George is in *Jumpers*, Moon keeps telling himself that he doesn't care.

In an imaginary press conference, Moon interviews himself about his reasons for carrying a bomb. He feels that civilization has gone out of control. Panic-stricken over the sheer volume and numbers of things and people multiplying madly, he believes that only an enormous explosion can shock the world into bringing life back down to a human scale. This reverie is interrupted by Lord Malquist, whose mention of gramophone records is the first specific indication that the novel is set in modern times. Then the narrative zeroes in on the incongruous spectacle of the coach-and-pair careening through a London in which "there were cars parked down both sides of the street, and many more nosed each other out of sight towards a mechanical infinity beyond human dominion, all essentially alike as though the product of some monstrous spawn."

The approach taken thus far in the novel would appear to be surrealistic, but Stoppard insists on its realism: "I'd produced the cogs and springs, but nobody would believe it was a clock."[4] In a *New Yorker* interview (May 4, 1968), he elaborated:

The action of the novel takes place within twenty-four hours in contemporary London. The characters have a sort of eccentricity that moves them into a Surrealistic context, but the book isn't in the least Surrealistic. Nothing in it is unreal or distorted, although some of it is heightened to a degree of absurdity. I think that realism has room for absurdity. It's sort of a funny book. I wrote it to be funny.

Similarly, Lord Malquist tells Moon in the first chapter: "I look around me and I recoil from such disorder. We live amidst absurdity, so close to it that it escapes our notice. But if the sky were turned into a great mirror and we caught ourselves in it unawares, we should not be able to look each other in the face. Since we cannot hope for order, let us withdraw with style from the chaos."

For Stoppard, style is cleverness, and cleverness is funny. His cleverness manifests itself not only in a profusion of bons mots and literary spoofs, but also in his deft orchestration of an improbable clutch of characters. Episodic characters are interpolated: Jane's French maid Marie, who spends most of the book under the sofa after being shot; the black Irish (Negro!) coachman O'Hara, with Jewish dialect and anti-Semitic sentiments, who serves as a pretext for Stoppard's mockery of religious and ethnic bigotry; the crusty old General, who photographs women in intimate detail and is killed in the act by Moon; and Birdboot, who is Lord Malquist's butler in livery. At the end of Chapter 2, "A Couple of Deaths and Exits," Moon commits two more irreversible actions; he inadvertently burns his notebook, and he releases the twelve-hour time fuse on his bomb.

Chapter 3, "Chronicler of the Time," is a pastiche of Samuel Pepys' diary; it is Moon's journal entry for the day, restating in a new perspective all the events that had occurred thus far. Chapter 4, "Spectator as Hero," begins with Moon rolling up the bodies of

Marie and the General in a carpet and loading them onto the Risen Christ's donkey to be carted aimlessly about London. Moon receives a number of wounds in the course of his peregrinations between his house and that of Lord Malquist. When he gets cut over the eye by the shattering glass of a mirror Jane throws at him, Moon suddenly experiences the same inner calm that the man in the story "Reunion" expected to achieve with a gratuitous act: "Moon exhaled as if his body were one big lung. The spring unwound itself, proportion was re-established. . . . He knew what it was to solve the world." One wound carries a religious connotation: when he cuts his finger while opening a can of pork and beans for the Risen Christ, Moon's blood soaks into the white bread, an evocation of the body and blood (bread and wine) of Christ. Moon later cuts the bottom of one foot, the heel of "his only remaining unwounded foot," and his left hand, and he is scratched by the lion. All together, these wounds have been taken to represent wounds to the psyche of the little man beset by forces beyond his control.

In Chapter 5, "The Funeral of the Year," the paths of all the major characters, as well as of the donkey and the lion, cross again, while the long, elaborate funeral cortège of a national hero (possibly Winston Churchill) passes in the background. The cowboys shoot each other in a showdown in Trafalgar Square, observed from the coach by Lord Malquist and Jane. To Moon's surprise, his bomb begins to play the National Anthem and to extrude an expanding red balloon from its nozzle. The balloon grows to the size of a church dome, displaying a two-word obscenity painted across it. At the end of the anthem it explodes, and a few funeral-procession spectators applaud. This cityscape recalls those of the French visionary Lautréamont.

Moon's sense of futility increases further when he returns to Lord Malquist's house, where the furniture is being tagged for sale to pay off creditors. A letter threatening Lord Malquist's life has arrived from the husband of the woman run over by his coach. Jane seems to have committed herself wholly to her aristocratic beau. The tenderness Moon has begun to feel toward Lady Malquist is squelched by her preference for the Risen Christ. Moon staggers, bleeding from all his wounds, out into the rain. O'Hara charitably puts him in the coach to take him home, but en route a bomb is thrown inside and lands in Moon's lap. Moon looks out the window, recognizes the revenge-bent husband, and catches the "look of apologetic concern" on his face just before the coach blows up, "dispersing Moon and O'Hara and bits of pink and yellow wreckage at various points along the road between the Palace and Parliament Square."

The 1966 novel offers numerous points of comparison with other works by Stoppard, most notably with his 1972 play, *Jumpers*. The apparent but unprovable infidelity of the wives of Moon and George Moore has been noted. The state funeral forms a backdrop to the action of the novel like the moon-landing and election victory in *Jumpers*. In the novel the funeral of the great statesman, "a leader who raised involvement to the level of sacred duty," marks the passing of an age. The future will belong, it seems, to "the Stylist, the spectator as hero." An indirect expression of the ascendancy of the spectator as hero in *Jumpers* is Dotty's reliance upon her television set and Jumper's use of the television camera to explore Dotty. George, too, avoids involvement when Clegthorpe is shot.

There are clear parallels between Sir Archibald Jumper and George Moore in *Jumpers* and the title characters of the novel, the elegantly fashionable Lord Malquist and the ineffectually cerebral Moon. Both Moore and Moon stand for moral values in a society that is visibly going awry with the abandonment of those values, but both are caught up in trivial considerations of their own making and are unable to perceive the grand design of things. Neither Moon's bomb nor Moore's lecture with visual aids can effect any change. It is Sir Archibald and Lord Malquist, both Stylists, who triumph, since they are able to detach themselves from the surrounding chaos. Other similarities between Moon and Moore are pointed out by Julian Gitzen in his article, "Tom Stoppard: Chaos in Perspective" (*Southern Humanities Review*, 1976):

Like Moon [Moore] is absentminded and perpetually losing and searching for something. He too is so openminded that he vacillates from one intellectual position to another. Moon's great unwritten work is a history of the world, while Moore's is a philosophical treatise which would have been called *The Concept of Knowledge*. . . . Moon is never fully able to comprehend what is taking place around him, while Moore remains ignorant until the end of the play of a murder committed in his own house at the beginning.

Moon's fears about the swelling tide of people and things that seems to be engulfing life on earth are similar to sentiments expressed in *Albert's Bridge*. Climbing the suspension bridge to get free of the noise and chaos, Fraser finds that "from a vantage point like this, the idea of society is just about tenable"—an integration of Moon's bewilderment with Lord Malquist's stylish solution ("When the battle becomes a farce the only position of dignity is above it"). Moon's apprehensions also recall Rosencrantz and Guildenstern's sense of helplessness when they are caught up in court intrigues they do not understand, and many of Moon's thought processes would apply as well to them: "The barriers, which protected him as long as he didn't acknowledge them, knocked each other over and his mind, caught unawares again, was overrun."

Hamlet is paid tribute in the novel, with its references to Lord Malquist's book in progress about book titles that had been excerpted from Shakespeare's text. Other literary borrowings foreshadow their more self-consciously proclaimed use in *Travesties*. Moon's walk from his own house to Lord Malquist's in "Spectator as Hero" is a pretext for a detailed description of "the labyrinthine muddle of London's streets," in the manner of James Joyce's writing about Dublin. The wit of Oscar Wilde echoes through many of Lord Malquist's epigrams: "If life is the pursuit of perfection than imperfection is the nature of life." "Let it be said of me that I was born appalled, lived disaffected, and died in the height of fashion." Critics have also detected the influences of Kingsley Amis, Salvador Dali, T.S. Eliot, Evelyn Waugh, and P.G. Wodehouse in *Lord Malquist and Mr Moon*.

Stoppard's one novel to date is, in sum, competently written and intellectually intriguing, although not startlingly original. The heavy-handedness of the scatological humor in proportion to other, more subtle, comic devices marks it as the work of a young writer. Since Stoppard has matured as a playwright since *Rosencrantz and Guildenstern Are Dead,* which came out at the same time as *Lord Malquist and Mr Moon,* it is reasonable to suppose that a new novel from Stoppard's hand would be a literary event. It is much harder, however, to find contemporary plays of the quality of Stoppard's full-length works for the stage than it is to find promising first novels like *Lord Malquist and Mr Moon.* We can be grateful that Stoppard has chosen to write for the theater.

5

Boots and Moons: Short Comedies, Radio Plays, Screenplays, and Translations

The connotative values of the words "boot" and "moon" range from the trivial to the sublime. Thus, although few of the works covered in this chapter stray very far toward the sublime end of the spectrum, these two recurrent words in Stoppard's vocabulary serve as an appropriate referent for the potpourri of short comedies, radio plays, screenplays, and translations that fill out Stoppard's canon. Before discussing these varied works, it may be appropriate to explore a thematic network of boots and moons in works already analyzed.

Stoppard is frequently asked why he has named so many of his characters Moon ("a person to whom things happen," Stoppard says) or Boot ("rather more aggressive").[1] His answers sound facetious, but reflect the fact that the creative process really defies explanation. He says that he cannot help it if that is what their names turn out to be. "All I know is if you're writing a play and somebody ought to be called Boot and is called Murgatroyd, it's impossible to continue."[2] He told one interviewer that he gave the name Moon to one of the critics in *The Real Inspector Hound* because he had just been to see the Paul Newman film *Left-Handed Gun*, in which some drunken cowboys shoot at the reflection of the moon in a horse trough, while Newman shouts the name of a character called Moon.[3] Even if this off-the-cuff story explains the origin of the name, Stoppard's predisposition toward the word is evident in the titles of two earlier plays, *M is for Moon Among Other Things* (1964) and *Another Moon Called Earth* (1967).

Stoppard's use of the name Boot can be more clearly traced. When Stoppard was drama critic for the understaffed *Scene* magazine, he also contributed pieces he felt ought not be published under the same name. These he signed "William Boot," a pseudonym borrowed from Evelyn Waugh's novel *Scoop*. The character, according to Stoppard, was "a journalist who brought a kind of innocent incompetence and contempt to what he was doing. . . . I used it, and got quite fond of Boot as a name."[4] Boot appears in a 1964 radio play, *The Dissolution of Dominic Boot*, and in an unpublished, unproduced ninety-minute television play, *This Way Out with Samuel Boot* (1964). A variation, Birdboot, is used for the other critic in *The Real Inspector Hound* and for Lord Malquist's butler in *Lord Malquist and Mr Moon*.

"I'm a Moon myself," Stoppard has confessed. "Confusingly, I used the name Boot, from Evelyn Waugh, as a pseudonym in journalism, but that was because Waugh's Boot is really a Moon, too." Kenneth Tynan also quotes English critic Robert Cushman's perception of Boot and Moon in *Rosencrantz and Guildenstern Are Dead*:

Rosencrantz, being eager, well-meaning, and consistently oppressed or embarrassed by every situation in which he finds himself, is clearly a Moon; Guildenstern, equally oppressed though less embarrassed and taking refuge in displays of intellectual superiority, is as obviously a Boot.[5]

Perhaps Cushman goes too far in second-guessing Stoppard's intentions, because these personality designations are reversed in *The Real Inspector Hound,* in which Moon is the ambitious pseudointellectual, while Birdboot's sensual nature frequently causes him embarrassment. The dichotomy, however, is accurate, and it obviously applies to characters in *Jumpers* and *Travesties* as well.

Boot and Moon are not only used as character names; the words crop up throughout Stoppard's works. For example, among Lord Malquist's frequent references to the importance of boots is a story he tells Jane:

The most honourable death I have ever heard of was that of Colonel Kelly of the Foot Guards who died in an attempt to save his boots from the Customs House fire. Colonel Kelly's boots were the envy of the town, they shone so. His friends hearing of his death rushed in their grief to buy the services of the valet who had the secret of the inimitable blacking. Now *that* is a tribute to an officer and a gentleman. . . .

A variant of "boot" is "foot," used as a character name in *After Magritte,* and as, undoubtedly, the part of the body most often mentioned in Stoppard's writing. Dotty in *Jumpers* and Albert in *Albert's Bridge* both sing medleys of songs about the moon. Also, in both *Jumpers* and in *Lord Malquist and Mr Moon,* the moon is mentioned as an ideal vantage point for an Olympian perspective on earthly chaos.

It is difficult to achieve an Olympian perspective on Stoppard's miscellany of minor works, but they are clearly related to those discussed in more detail in earlier chapters. The plays included in this chapter come from the entire span of Stoppard's career as a dramatist, beginning with his first full-length play *A Walk on the Water* (1963), revised in 1968 as *Enter A Free Man,* and ending with the one-act *Dogg's Hamlet* (1979). The latter play's companion piece, *Cahoot's Macbeth,* is discussed in the chapter on political plays. Other plays considered here are *The Real Inspector Hound*, (1968), *After Magritte* (1970), *Dogg's Our Pet* (1971), *Dirty Linen/New-Found-Land* (1976), and *The (15 Minute) Dogg's Troupe Hamlet* (1976).

Stoppard's characteristic style is not fully developed in *Enter A Free Man*, but the play does contain many of the ideas and situations that are used with greater finesse in later plays. George Riley is the first of Stoppard's ineffectual dreamers, all of whom are passively tolerated or even humored in their delusions by their wives, who are more in touch with reality. Like George Moore in *Jumpers*, Moon in *Lord Malquist and Mr Moon* and in *The Real Inspector Hound*, and Carr in *Travesties*, Riley is a man of unrealized ambition. He moves back and forth between the living room of his home and an old-fashioned neighborhood pub, in a simultaneous setting like the ones in *Jumpers* and *Travesties*.

The first scene in the pub contains two of Stoppard's favorite devices: a confusion of names (a nondescript bar patron named Brown is called Smith, Green, Jones, and Robinson) and game-playing (a spy game and a courtroom trial game, in which Riley is virtually the only player). Late in the play there is a reversal of the audience's assumptions about characters' names, when it is revealed that Carmen the barman is really named Victor, that Able the seaman is really Richard, and that Riley's wife Persephone is really Constance (she never learns about Riley's fantasy name for her).

Sounds are used to good effect, even supplying symbolic overtones. There is the drone of Riley's wife's Hoover, the mindless chatter of his daughter's radio, and his own invention—a grandfather clock that plays "Rule, Britannia" every noon and midnight, disrupting the family's sleep.

George Riley is an inventor who never made any money from his inventions. He was supported first by his wife, who runs their tidy little house, and now his way is paid by his eighteen-year-old daughter Linda, who sells cosmetics at Woolworth's and gives him ten shillings a week to spend at the pub. Act 1 illustrates the Riley family's unchanging pattern of life. Linda is rebellious and unsentimental, but longs for commitment to a man. Her latest in a long series of brief relationships is with a man who rides a motorcycle. She spends a day taken off from work, lounging about in pyjamas, ordering her mother to bring tea, and allowing her to sweep up the crumbs. While sweeping, Persephone defends Riley's lack of achievement, and, each evening, she lays a place for him at the table, even when he has announced that this time he really is leaving home for good.

Riley habitually announces his own entrance into the pub: "Enter a free man!" His latest invention is an envelope with glue on both sides of the flap so that it can be turned inside out and reused. Harry, one of the regular patrons, strings him along, leading Riley to believe that they will go into partnership to produce these envelopes. Able, a sailor, seems genuinely impressed with Riley. Florence enters just after the exit of Harry, whom she was to have met there. Riley mistakes her warm friendliness for consent to run away with him and find a new life, financed by his anticipated business partnership. He rejects the domestic coziness that has stifled his "creative spirit" and says he will meet Florence in the pub the next day.

In Act 2, Linda and Riley fight over her intention to go off with the motorcyclist and over his refusal to register for unemployment compensation. Then he gently tells Persephone that this time he is not only leaving home but also taking up with another woman,

one with whom he had developed a spiritual understanding. He enters the pub in high spirits, which are
soon dashed by the realization that Florence belongs to
Harry and that Harry never intended to form a partnership. The reusable envelope is an unworkable invention, because the envelope gets torn after the first mail-
ing. Even Able laughingly expresses disillusionment
with Riley, who did not even know his "partner's" last
name.

At home, Linda tells Persephone that she came
back from her attempted elopement because, halfway
to Scotland, she learned that the motorcyclist was already married; she had not even known his real name.
The one who does know her man is Persephone; she
knew that Riley would be back, and she has his supper
ready. Just then, another of Riley's inventions begins to
go awry. His system of indoor rain for Persephone's
plants has no shut-off provision. Buckets and saucepans
are placed under the drips. Linda gives Riley more
money. Life in the household will continue unchanged.

Riley's impracticality, combined with his insistence upon his creative spirit, suggests that he represents the artist—a being apart from the mainstream of
society. Linda says that "he's living in a dreamland,"
and, referring to his habit of reading all her old
children's books, tells him to "stop living in my childhood." The fact that he does not pay his own way may
mean that he is a product of Stoppard's guilt feelings
about being an artist. As Stoppard said in the longer
passage quoted in Chapter 3, artists "operate not precisely at the hub of society" and "don't in fact contribute in a way that one can contribute a bicycle or a
pound of butter."[6] Pursuing this interpretation, Florence may represent the artist's muse. Even her name,
Florence Lawrence (which is, incidentally, the name of
the first silent screen actress to have her identity re-

vealed to the public), is already rhymed, anticipating Riley's need to invent a cognomen.

A more comprehensive interpretation of the play is that it comments upon social structures in England. Within the middle-class milieu of the play, there exists a microcosm of the larger society. Riley's home—with its "Rule, Britannia" clock, its portrait of the Queen on the wall, and its constant routine—symbolizes that society. Riley says of it, "I sometimes think of myself as a sailor, in a way. . .with home as a little boat, anchored in the middle of a big calm sea, never going anywhere, just sitting, far from land, life, everything. . . ." In this context, Riley represents the leisured class, clinging to its ideals but remaining nonproductive. Understood in this light, there is particular poignancy in Riley's perception of his own life, "when a man's past outweighs his future." His nostalgia for vanishing values is reinforced in speeches such as this:

RILEY: Dreams! The illusion of something for nothing. No wonder the country is going to the dogs. Personal enterprise sacrificed to bureaucracy. No pride, no patriotism. The erosion of standards, the spread of mediocrity, the decline of craftsmanship and the betrayal of the small inventor.

Persephone, by this interpretation, represents the laboring classes, the steady, untiring backbone of the household. Linda is the current generation of youth that tends to subvert traditional values. Spoiled and lazy, she works mainly to acquire material possessions and immediate gratifications. Persephone tells her, "I've kept our life tidy—I've looked after you, and him, and got you this far—perhaps it is a waste of time." There is a somewhat threadbare use of this allegory of a larger society in passages like this:

LINDA: . . . You and me, we're the Society for the Preservation of George Riley! God, if his father hadn't died, he wouldn't even have a house to live in!

PERSEPHONE: You want to know what he was like—? He was a gentleman. (*Pause.*) You'd better call him—and tell him to wash his hands. He usually forgets.

LINDA (*getting up*): Gentleman George. . . . (*At door.*) Dad!

Ronald Hayman compares *Enter A Free Man* to Henrik Ibsen's *The Wild Duck*, since both plays revolve around a self-deceiving, middle-aged man who allows his wife and daughter to support him. Hayman then comments:

Enter A Free Man light-heartedly develops the theme of the life-lie without depending on solidly realized relationships between the characters. Realization of this sort could never have been Stoppard's forte and his development has carried him felicitously away from the need to depend on it. In most of his work the dazzling brightness of the comedy stops us from asking ourselves 'Is this relationship convincing?'[7]

Stoppard's opinion of his own characters in this play agrees with Hayman's estimation. He told an interviewer: "I don't think it's a very true play, in the sense that I feel no intimacy with the people I was writing about."[8] Nor is the comedy as dazzling in *Enter A Free Man* as audiences have subsequently come to expect from Stoppard, but it is a solidly crafted play. As a first play, it is competently written and stageworthy; as a point of departure for his subsequent playwriting career, it indicates how far and how fast Stoppard's talents have matured.

The Real Inspector Hound is a two-track spoof. It revels in the foibles and pomposities of theater critics, while at the same time burlesquing the classic country-manorhouse murder-mystery play. The two lines of development run parallel during much of the action, the clichés of one serving as counterpoint to the clichés of the other. They finally converge and loop around each other inextricably when each subject needs the other for the ingenious solution.

The setting is the drawing room of Muldoon Manor. Its atmosphere is detailed in some deliberately cumbersome expository dialogue. For example: "I took the short cut over the cliffs and followed one of the old smugglers' paths through the treacherous swamps that surround this strangely inaccessible house." "The fog is very treacherous around here—it rolls off the sea without warning, shrouding the cliffs in a deadly mantle of blind man's buff." The parody in such lines exploits the literary lode of Nancy Drew and Agatha Christie. A body is lying on the drawing-room floor when the curtain rises, and it remains there during the entire play, much of the time covered by a settee which the maid inadvertently moves.

At the back of this acting area, the theater audience perceives something like a mirror-reflection of itself. Actually, this is the seating for the audience-within-the-play, or what Randall Craig, in *Drama* (Autumn 1976), called "a play outside a play." When *The Real Inspector Hound* begins, the two front-center seats are taken by two theater critics, Moon and Birdboot. They begin a conversation that continues during the play-within-the-play and reveals greater preoccupation with themselves than with the performance they are reviewing.

Moon's overriding concern is that he is only the second-string critic of his newspaper. Spurred by the murder plot on stage, his thoughts lead him to fantasize about murdering his superior, Higgs, and he wonders whether third-string critic Puckeridge ever dreams of seeing both himself and Higgs dead. Birdboot, who munches chocolates during the play, has amorous inclinations toward the ingenue who plays Felicity. He urges Moon to review her favorably, but denies any personal involvement with her, although Moon had seen them together the night before. Midway through the performance, Birdboot finds himself more attracted to the mature actress playing Cynthia, Lady Muldoon. His fickleness is like that of the callous Simon, a character in the thriller, who also switches from Felicity to Cynthia.

When Moon and Birdboot do make critical comments on the production, their dialogue is riddled with jargon. Birdboot's banal approach is subjective and effusive: ". . . one of the summits in the range of contemporary theatre." "—the radiance, the inner sadness—," "It is at this point that the play, for me, comes alive," and ". . . a good clean show without a trace of smut." Moon's style, on the other hand, is pretentious and nonsensically analytical:

Je suis, it seems to be saying, *ergo sum*. But is that enough? I think we are entitled to ask. For what in fact is this play concerned with? It is concerned with what I have referred to elsewhere as the nature of identity.

. . . . .

If we examine this more closely, and I think close examination is the least tribute that this play deserves, I think we will find that within the austere framework of what is seen to be on one level a country-house week-end, and what a useful symbol that is, the author has given us—yes, I will go so far—he has given us the human condition—

. . . . .

Faced as we are with such ubiquitous obliquity, it is hard, it is hard indeed, and therefore I will not attempt to refrain from invoking the names of Kafka, Sartre, Shakespeare, St Paul, Beckett, Birkett, Pinero, Pirandello, Dante and Dorothy L. Sayers.

The play that inspires these opinions is a farrago of commonplaces of character, dialogue, and situation.

Mrs Drudge, the maid, provides most of the exposition by answering the telephone with lines like "the same, half an hour later," and turning on the radio always just when the police report is starting. She has a habit of entering silently, just in time to overhear each character in turn say: "I will kill you, Simon Gascoyne!"

Besides Felicity and Cynthia, the other occupant of the manor house is Magnus, Lord Muldoon's crippled half-brother "who turned up out of the blue from Canada just the other day." His wheelchair can be heard approaching down several flights of stairs, and he says lines like, "You are a damned attractive woman, Cynthia," and "Well, I think I'll go and oil my gun." The last character to appear is Inspector Hound. He comes to the manor in search of an escaped madman, but his interrogation unearths no clues.

In an article in *Modern Drama* (March 1977), Brian Crossley pinpoints a specific play within the murder-mystery genre: "*The Real Inspector Hound* finds its target in a contemporary play, that most famous of all stage whodunits, Agatha Christie's *The Mousetrap*. Stoppard's work parallels this popular play at virtually all its crucial points. For example, we are invited to discover 'who done it?' only to find that the detective plays two roles, sleuth and slayer."

Simon discovers the corpse while momentarily alone in the room. There is a shot, Simon falls dead, and the first act of the play-within-the-play is over. During intermission the telephone rings on stage. Birdboot answers it and expostulates against his wife for calling him at work. As he hangs up, Felicity enters, and Birdboot finds himself, in reacting to her, caught up in the play—repeating much of Simon's previous dialogue and business. It is Birdboot who discovers that the long-present corpse on stage is that of the critic Higgs. There is a shot, Birdboot falls dead, and Moon runs to him.

Before Moon can return to his seat, his place and Birdboot's are taken by Simon and Hound, whose comments on the play are scathingly unfavorable. Moon assumes the role of the Inspector, but then is forced to admit that he is not "the real Inspector Hound." Magnus rises from his wheelchair, removes his moustaches, and announces himself to be the real Inspector Hound. But Moon now recognizes the third-stringer Puckeridge—the murderer of Higgs. Puckeridge shoots Moon. Finally, we learn that Puckeridge/Hound/Magnus is also Cynthia's long-lost husband Albert, whose memory has just returned after years as an amnesiac. He and Cynthia embrace, while Moon dies saying, with a trace of admiration, "Puckeridge! . . . you cunning bastard."

Stoppard has said that the play is not *about* critics. He started it with the notion of having two audience members get involved in the play-within-the-play, and he ended up making them critics because this gave him a good target for parody.[9] He bore no grudge against critics, since he had not yet in his career experienced the emotionally devastating effect of bad reviews, although he had perhaps been disappointed by superficial ones. He did, however, show special insight into the feelings of theater people with his clever switching of roles—putting the critics on stage to be judged by actors in the critics' seats. That device capitalizes on the belief of actors and directors that, if the critics could only understand the creative process behind a production through practical involvement, their opinions would be more enlightened and meaningful. It is an actualization of the desire to say to critics, "If you think you know so much about theater, let's see what you can do." Thus, when Birdboot is put on stage he is accused of turning the thriller into a farce. Moon is simply incompetent on stage, unable to assume the role of Inspector Hound.

What the play is about, according to Stoppard, is the dangers of wish fulfillment. Birdboot plays Simon's role in order to win Cynthia and is shot, like Simon. Moon's wish to see Higgs dead comes true, but he too must die at the hands of the jealous, ambitious critic below him. If this is truly what the play is *about*, then the work is rather flimsy, for this theme is not readily apparent, nor is it developed in any way or treated on any level other than that of situation. The play might just as easily be about the delights of wish fulfillment as about its dangers. If Stoppard's audience wishes to enjoy the tried and true aspects of an Agatha Christie play along with the satisfaction of feeling superior to her audience, then its wish will be fulfilled.

Another subject of *The Real Inspector Hound* is the difficulty of determining the boundary between art and life. When the critics' own lives become enmeshed in the action of the play, one must admire the sheer technical virtuosity by which one's attention is led back and forth across that boundary. Whether Stoppard was consciously building upon Pirandello's technique of forcing the spectator constantly to reexamine his assumptions about different levels of reality, or whether he was merely spoofing Pirandello for the amusement of the cognoscenti, it is in this regard that the play best succeeds.

It has become fairly common practice to produce *After Magritte* as a curtain-raiser (or afterpiece) to *The Real Inspector Hound*. Written two years after the longer one-act, in 1970, *After Magritte* complements it well, since both plays feature a police inspector's investigation of an ill-defined crime. They differ in stylistic approach and in entertainment values. *After Magritte* is the less successful of the two, but it merits brief consideration, because it is the clearest example of a certain unspontaneous, studied lunacy that recurs in Stoppard's work. *After Magritte* may also have been

Stoppard's most conscious effort to develop the visual element of his theatre to a parity with its verbal complexity.

After Magritte proceeds from a good idea, but it quickly degenerates into self-conscious cleverness. The title, which implies that it is done in imitation of the surrealist painter Magritte, and the stage picture at the start of the play lead one to expect a surrealist work. Surrealism is an artistic credo that seeks to transcend reality through the use of unconscious dream images and other irrational imaginings. But Stoppard's paradoxical introduction of a controlling element of logic in *After Magritte* makes of the whole a rather tedious exercise in shortchanging the imagination. The appeal of Magritte's paintings is that one cannot supply banal realistic explanations for his haunting images. Stoppard reduces the images to commonplaces, and although one may enjoy the schoolboy humor of it, the ultimate response is "Is that all?"

Just as Stoppard has used works by other writers (Shakespeare, Wilde, Christie) as skeletal supports for his plays, so he bases this one on the work of another artist—a painter, this time, instead of a playwright. According to Wendell V. Harris, "the opening scene is almost certainly modelled on Magritte's '*L'Assassin menacé*' (1926)."[10] When the play begins, all of the furniture in the room is stacked up against the door to the street. The ceiling light fixture is on a cord that is counterweighted by a basket of fruit hanging from another cord. Harris stands on a chair under the light fixture and blows at it; he wears black evening-dress trousers tucked into thigh-high rubber fishing boots, but his torso is bare. His wife Thelma, in a ballgown, crawls about the floor and sniffs. Mother lies on the ironing board, one foot against the electric iron; she wears a black rubber bathing cap and is covered by a towel, upon which a black bowler hat is placed. Outside the window, Police Constable Holmes stands gazing into the room, motionless until Thelma closes the curtains. Scattered about the floor are .22 lead slugs. All of these things have perfectly rational and innocent explanations that come out gradually in the course of the play, but will not be elaborated here.

Earlier that day the family had gone to see an exhibition of Magritte's paintings at the Tate Gallery (which was actually held there, February 14 to March 30, 1969). They went because Mother plays the tuba, and she had heard that many of Magritte's paintings include tubas. Also common in the paintings are derby hats, light bulbs, chairs, tables, and windows—the props of *After Magritte*.

As the family drove away from the gallery they saw something that each of them interpreted differently. Harris saw a man in pyjamas with a white beard, holding a tortoise under one arm and brandishing a blind man's white cane. Thelma saw a one-legged football player with shaving cream on his face, carrying a football (or a wineskin or bagpipes) and an ivory cane. Mother saw a man with a surgical mask on his face wearing the loose-fitting gaberdine of a convicted felon, carrying a handbag and waving a cricket bat as he played hopscotch. When Inspector Foot arrives, he repeats a secondhand eyewitness account of a minstrel player carrying a crocodile boot and a broken crutch.

By a farfetched sequence of deductions based upon the sketchy eyewitness report, Foot has concluded that there was a robbery. Since he himself had noticed a car with a yellow parking ticket on the windshield, he traced the ticket to Harris's home, expecting to find an accomplice. Police Constable Holmes, meanwhile, through the window had seen Mother in her black bathing cap on the ironing board with the derby hat on her stomach, and reported "an illegal operation on a bald nigger minstrel" performed without an anaesthetic. Again, there is a logical explanation for what the family had seen and for the discovery that it was Foot himself who had been observed by so many witnesses. Finally, the audience knows in advance the reasons for the even more bizarre tableau that closes the play.

Like *After Magritte, Dirty Linen* is a bit of fluff. Its flimsy structure exists only to support jokes—puns, double entendres, sight gags—all on a single subject: sex in high places. Since much of the verbal humor depends upon timing and inflection, *Dirty Linen* can be a far better play when seen in production than the text would suggest. This play and *New-Found-Land,* the companion piece it contains, were directed with great verve and inventiveness in both their London and New York premieres by Ed Berman, for whom the plays were written.

American-born Berman went to Oxford as a Rhodes Scholar in the early 1960s, after graduating from Harvard. He liked England well enough to stay there, and in 1968 he founded Inter-Action, a charitable trust whose purpose is to stimulate community involvement in the arts. In addition to Inter-Action's work in schools, youth clubs, mental hospitals, community centers, and playgrounds, and such projects as City Farms I in Kentish Town, it sponsors theatrical productions under several headings: the Ambiance Lunch Hour Theatre Club (which staged the premiere of *After Magritte* in 1970), the Almost Free Theatre, the Fun Art Bus, Dogg's Troupe, and, since 1979, the British American Repertory Company.

To celebrate the American Bicentennial as well as his own imminent naturalization as a British citizen, Berman planned a series of productions grouped under the title "The American Connection" at his lunch-hour theatre. Stoppard agreed to contribute a play, and started *Dirty Linen* with the idea that it would be in the form of a committee meeting to debate Berman's application for British citizenship. *Dirty Linen*, however, went off in another direction when Stoppard used a variation of an old idea, rather than an American subject. Luckily, Stoppard had a last-minute flash of inspiration: "I realized that all I had to do was to have an adjournment, put in fifteen minutes about America, and I'd solved Berman's problem as well."[11]

Dirty Linen and *New-Found-Land* are set in a House of Commons committee meeting room in the tower of Big Ben. The first to enter is a very attractive young woman named Maddie Gotobed. She carries a small sack from a modish lingerie shop, out of which—after verifying that she is alone—she takes a pair of French silk knickers (panties) with distinctive red lace trimmings, and puts them on.

As the committee members gradually arrive and introduce themselves to her, it becomes clear that each of them—unknown to the others—has been intimate with her. Two of them surreptitiously return to her lace panties they have brought in a briefcase or suit pocket. Another passes her a note asking her to forget their recent rendezvous. Another receives his own briefs back from Maddie in an envelope. He quickly stuffs them away, setting up a joke that comes later in the action:

> "What is that?"
> "Pair of briefs."
> "What are they doing in there?"
> "It's a briefcase."

The Select Committee on Promiscuity in High Places has been constituted in response to press reports that no fewer than 119 members of Parliament have been involved with the same woman, an unknown seductress who has been "going through the ranks like a lawn-mower in knickers." The audience has no trouble deciding who the mystery woman is, especially when it learns that Maddie has become the committee's clerk (an overnight promotion from the Home Office typing pool), and that her secretarial talents were probably not the deciding factor:

COMMITTEE CHAIRMAN: You do speedwriting, I suppose?
MADDIE: Yes, if I'm given enough time.

They accommodate her stenographic speed in a very funny sequence in which the debate is carried out in slow motion.

Maddie keeps losing articles of clothing—skirt, slip, blouse—in the course of the meeting, but this does not inhibit her interjection of her own opinions into the proceedings. Needless to say, she has more common sense than any of them. This, by the way, is the full extent of the thought content of the play:

People don't care what M.P.s do in their spare time, they just want them to do their jobs properly bringing down prices and everything. . . . Why don't they have a Select Committee to report on what M.P.s have been up to in their *working* hours—that's what people want to know.

. . . . .

The press. The more you accuse them of malice and inaccuracy, the more you're admitting that they've got a right to poke their noses into your private life. All this fuss! The whole report can go straight in the waste-paper basket. All you need is one paragraph saying that M.P.s have got just as much right to enjoy themselves in their own way as anyone else, and Fleet Street can take a running jump.

The committee's deliberations are well underway when its last member arrives. French, surprisingly, does not seem to be acquainted with Maddie. Furthermore, it appears that he is going to make trouble for the committee. In a united stand by which they hope to confuse the issue, all the other members—including the one woman M.P.—confess transgressions. Just then the Division Bell sounds and the meeting is adjourned for ten minutes so that they can go and vote. Momentarily left alone with French, Maddie asks him to show her the way to the ladies' cloakroom. They exit together.

"As soon as the door closes," the stage directions say, "the other opens and two men enter—but they are in another play." The two characters in *New-Found-Land* are Arthur, a very junior Home Office official, and Bernard, a very senior Home Office official. They had been looking for an empty room in which to work. Before they can settle down, Bernard shows Arthur an ancient five-pound note and launches into a long story, which Arthur has obviously heard before, about how as a young man he won it in a bet with Prime Minister Lloyd George. The effect of the story, although Bernard does not make a point of it, is to show that sexual promiscuity has occurred in high places at least as far back as the Great War.

Arthur presses forward the naturalization papers that they are to consider. The description of the applicant fits Ed Berman exactly:

ARTHUR: There's a theatrical side to him.

BERNARD: Do you mean he waves his arms around?

ARTHUR: No—no—he writes plays, and puts them on and so on. He seems to have some kind of theatre.

BERNARD: Oh dear, yes. A theatrical farmer with buses on the side, doing publishing and community work in a beard . . .

Bernard makes a few generalizations about the American national character. Arthur responds with a six-page monologue about the scenic wonders and regional color of the United States, during which Bernard falls asleep.

Arthur's monologue is a virtuoso piece of writing, in that it manages to be at once both lyrical and funny.

Much of it sounds like tourist-brochure hyperbole, but there are such telling details as the "fried chicken and bottles of cherry soda" served in the deep South to a train car of "Bible salesmen, buck privates from Fort Dixie, majorettes from L.S.U., farm boys, and a couple of nuns." The speech probably effects a surge of nostalgic recognition in American audiences, for in general, American reviewers wrote more favorably of *New-Found-Land* than of *Dirty Linen*, whereas British opinion was usually the reverse. Edwin Wilson's description in the *Wall Street Journal* (December 13, 1976) is a good example of the American reaction:

Beginning with the arrival of a foreigner on a ship near the "Brooklyn Bay Bridge" and the Statue of Liberty, it moves by train—the Chattanooga Choo Choo—through a mythical America—New York, New England, Chicago, Kentucky, New Orleans, and the West Coast—evoking words and images of Walt Whitman, Mark Twain, Tin Pan Alley, advertising slogans, and old movies. In sentences rivaling anything in a Thomas Wolfe novel, it goes on for ten minutes. Tour-de-force hardly describes the speech; it is one of the most brilliant, sparkling sustained passages ever written about America as seen through popular myths and clichés.

At the end of Arthur's flight of rhetorical fancy, the committee members from *Dirty Linen* burst into the room and that play resumes.

Matters are resolved very quickly in the short final segment of *Dirty Linen*. The Home Secretary arrives to consult with Bernard and Arthur just as the Select Committee is reconvening. He signs Berman's application with a flourish, saying "One more American can't make any difference." Bernard takes out his five-pound note and starts to tell his Lloyd George story, but the committee chairman snatches the note and tears it into four pieces. The intruders leave, and the Select Committee settles down. French announces that during the adjournment he has drafted a committee report to the

Prime Minister. He reads from a paper the very opinions Maddie had expressed earlier. It is accepted unanimously. The play ends with French pulling from his pocket to wipe his brow—instead of a handkerchief—the pair of knickers that Maddie had put on at the beginning.

The entire intermissionless evening of theatre, which one critic calls *Dirty (New-Found-Land) Linen*, runs about ninety minutes. Although billed as two separate plays that happen to use the same set, there is a certain built-in interdependence. Of the two, the very short *New-Found-Land* could more easily be performed independently as a one-act play, since its only textual link with the longer play is Bernard's mention of French. *Dirty Linen* cannot stand alone, as it needs the break in its action in order to prepare the denouement; a regular intermission would be inappropriate, since the remainder of the play is less than ten minutes long. The business with the five-pound note and the naturalization papers at the end of *Dirty Linen* would be meaningless without *New-Found-Land*. Even if these are two separate plays, the work is unified and coherent.

Nevertheless, *Dirty Linen* is not to everyone's taste. Although most reviewers claimed to have laughed uproariously at the performance, Martin Gottfried (*New York Post*, January 12, 1977) probably expressed the verdict of posterity when he called it "undergraduate satire." Walter Kerr (*New York Times*, January 23, 1977) called it "altogether intolerable" and went on to explain: "Wide-ranging as his antic interests are, delightful as his impish mismatches can occasionally be, his management of them is essentially slovenly. He rarely peels a top layer away to see if there might be something better underneath." Stoppard purposely avoids peeling the onion—with this particular play, at least. He told interviewer Robert B. Semple (*New York*

Times, June 21, 1976): "My director thinks he's got a profound comment on British society. What he really has is a knickers farce." Berman had a success with the play and was naturalized on the day of its first performance, April 5, 1976.

It was also for Berman that Stoppard wrote three other equally insubstantial playlets: *Dogg's Our Pet* (1971), *The (15 Minute) Dogg's Troupe Hamlet* (1976), and *Dogg's Hamlet* (1979). Although written during an eight-year period, these very short pieces have certain overlapping characteristics. The most recent of these one-act plays is the first half of a full-length bill called *Dogg's Hamlet/Cahoot's Macbeth*, which uses truncated versions of the two Shakespearean plays as points of departure. (As mentioned earlier, *Cahoot's Macbeth* is distinct enough in tone and purpose to be classed with the "political plays" discussed in Chapter 6.) *Dogg's Hamlet* is itself composed of two parts: the first section repeats a linguistic experiment Stoppard had conducted in *Dogg's Our Pet*, uses the same characters, and even incorporates some speeches verbatim from the earlier play; the second half of *Dogg's Hamlet* is, with only minute revisions, *The (15 Minute) Dogg's Troupe Hamlet*.

Stoppard acknowledges Wittgenstein's *Philosophical Investigation* as the source of his idea for *Dogg's Our Pet*. A more accessible influence is René Magritte, who is quoted in the catalogue of the 1969 Tate Gallery exhibition of his works: "No object is so attached to its name that another cannot be found which suits it better."[12] Two languages are used in *Dogg's Our Pet*. One is English, the other is composed mostly of English words that mean something other than the meaning assigned by English-speakers.

Charlie, a workman, is building a platform composed of wood in various shapes and sizes, which are tossed to him by an unseen offstage helper. Unknown to Charlie, his helper speaks a language in which "plank," "slab," "block," "brick," and "cube" mean, respectively, "Here!," "Ready!," "Next!," the name of the unseen helper, and "Thank you!" This semantic difference does not interfere with the progress of the work, even when two schoolboys—Able and Baker —enter, playing ball in Brick's language. Game-playing seems to transcend language barriers, as evidenced by Charlie's ability to share in the boys' fun while he works.

Professor Dogg, the boys' headmaster, enters and hands out small flags to members of the audience, counting them out from one to twelve: "sun, dock, trog, slack, pan, sock, bright, nun, tun, what, dunce." Now Charlie's incomprehension causes the platform-building activity to slow down. Despite various complications, the structure is somehow completed, and there are enough blocks and slabs left over to build a wall. The lettering on these blocks spells: DOGG POUT THERE END. The wall is repeatedly knocked down and rebuilt, so that the same letters become SHOUT DOGG PERT NEED and DONT UPSET DOGG HERE. (The play's title, *Dogg's Our Pet*, is also an anagram—for Dogg's Troupe.)

Dogg hooks a ribbon across the platform and unrolls a red carpet. A Lady enters—"perhaps she is the Queen, or perhaps the wife of the Chairman of the Board of Governors." She bravely mounts the wobbly platform and, in ladylike tones, delivers her speech— "Scabs, slobs, black yobs, yids, spicks, wops . . . " —which culminates in the cutting of the ribbon, as she declares, "Sod the pudding club!"

After the dignitaries have left, Charlie, who heretofore used only monosyllabic sentences, cannot resist having his say from the platform. His main point is: "I can take a joke as well as any man, but I've noticed a lot of language about the place and if there's one thing

I can't stand it's language." Then he reassembles the wall to read: DOGGS TROUPE THE END.

There is a certain fascination, also exploited by David Storey's *The Contractor* (1969), in watching something usable being assembled on stage. In *Dogg's Our Pet*, the audience sees that a language is constructed in much the same way as a platform. As an intellectual exercise, however, the play's linguistic games descend to the level of anagrams. And, as an experiment in theatre, *Dogg's Our Pet* (like the first half of *Dogg's Hamlet*) is roughly as satisfying to its audience as the experience of watching a game of charades one is not allowed to play.

In the 1979 play *Dogg's Hamlet*, Charlie is a schoolboy like Able and Baker, and they all speak Dogg's language. They and headmaster Dogg are preparing for the performance of a school play in its original language, English, which is a foreign language to them. They rehearse random lines from *Hamlet* in halting English.

A load of blocks and planks is delivered by Easy, an English-speaking truck driver, who helps the boys construct their stage. From this point on, the action is similar to that of *Dogg's Our Pet*. The Lady's speech is the same, only this time her function is to award the school's trophies, all of which go to a teacher's pet named Fox. Mrs Dogg is there, too. With a curtsey she presents flowers to the Lady: "Hernia, suppurating kidneys, reeks catboils frankly gangrenous armpit dripping maggots." This sophomoric joke is the low point of the tedious business. The same point about the arbitrariness of social conventions assigned to words has been made with far more style and robustly universal good humor by Luis Buñuel in his film *The Phantom of Liberty*, or with more subtlety by Peter Handke in his play *Offending the Audience*.

Finally, Stoppard's characters are ready to perform their play-within-the-play. "The 15-Minute Hamlet" comes as much-needed relief within the context of *Dogg's Hamlet*. Professor Dogg enters, costumed as Shakespeare, to speak the Prologue:

> For this relief, much thanks.
> Though I am native here, and to the manner born,
> It is a custom more honoured in the breach
> Than in the observance
> Well.
> Something is rotten in the state of Denmark.
> To be, or not to be, that is the question.
> There are more things in heaven and earth
> Than are dreamt of in your philosophy—
> There's a divinity that shapes our ends,
> Rough hew them how we will
> Though this be madness, yet there is method in it.
> I must be cruel only to be kind;
> Hold, as t'were, the mirror up to nature
> A countenance more in sorrow than in anger.
>
> (LADY in audience shouts "Marmalade")
>
> The Lady doth protest too much.
> Cat will mew, and Dogg will have his day!

In the original 1976 text of "The 15-Minute Dogg's Hamlet," the Lady in the audience shouted "Rotten!" instead of "Marmalade," which is a sign of approbation in Dogg's language. Other revisions made in the text, for incorporation within the longer 1979 play, are mainly added indications of stage business and of some laughably claptrap scenic effects, such as a cardboard moon that flaps up and down frenetically to distinguish night from day scenes. According to the earlier text, the players were imaginary, and the court watched an imaginary play; in the later version, puppets are used.

Dogg reappears in the role of Claudius. Fox, the

school's star pupil, plays Hamlet. Abel is cast as Bernardo/Marcellus and as Laertes; Baker as Francisco/Horatio, Osric, and Fortinbras; Charlie as Ophelia; and Mrs Dogg as Gertrude. One other actor, playing the ghost and the gravedigger, completes the cast of "the 15-minute Hamlet." After racing through the highlights of Shakespeare's *Hamlet* in twelve or thirteen minutes, they do an encore—a two-minute condensation of it.

Ophelia's death is one of many madcap sight gags, especially in the speeded-up replaying of the action. She enters, falls to the ground, then pulls a gravestone to cover herself. The twelve-minute "Hamlet" ends with Fortinbras's line, "Go, bid the soldiers shoot," and four shots are heard from off stage; the encore ends with Hamlet's dying words "the rest is silence" and two offstage shots. The entire quarter-hour's foolishness is a miracle of compression, and it is very, very funny. Jack Kroll (*Newsweek*, September 24, 1979), the only New York critic to see a serious point to the proceedings, declared: "The joke's not on Shakespeare, but on the modern world's short-circuiting of human sensibility that Stoppard takes to its ultimate crazy logic." That interpretation, if arrived at by anyone in the audience, would make an appropriate transition into the mood of *Cahoot's Macbeth* on the second half of the bill.

At least two of Stoppard's radio plays, *Albert's Bridge* (1969) and *If You're Glad I'll be Frank* (1966), have been produced for the stage. These have been published in the United States along with three other radio plays: *A Separate Peace* (1966), *Where Are They Now?* (1970), and *Artist Descending A Staircase* (1972). Synopses of the unpublished radio and television plays are included in a checklist of works by and about Stoppard in *Theatrefacts* (May–June 1974); those titles are *The Dissolution of Dominic Boot* (radio, 1964), *Teeth* (television, 1967), *Another Moon Called Earth* (television, 1967), *Neutral Ground* (television, 1968), and *The Engagement* (television, 1970). The predominant themes that occur in these relatively early works are: the difficulty of achieving a harmonious working relationship between husband and wife on a psychological or a practical level; the loss of human values in a technological society and the destruction that follows persistent attempts to escape that society; the relative nature of truth, especially with regard to memories of the past. All of these themes are treated in Stoppard's more important works, and the radio plays will not repay exhaustive analysis here. However, special mention should be made of *Albert's Bridge*, the best-constructed radio play, and *If You're Glad I'll Be Frank*, Stoppard's closest approach to Theatre of the Absurd.

Albert is a college-educated young man who finds greater self-fulfillment in a summer job painting the Clufton Bay Bridge than he did in all his philosophy courses at the university. As he tells an elderly co-worker:

. . . your bargain with the world, your wages, your time, your energy, your property, everything you took out and everything you put in, the bargain that has carried you this far—all contained there in ten layers of paint, accounted for. Now that's something; to keep track of everything you put into the kitty, to have it lie there, under your eye, fixed and immediate—there are no consequences to a coat of paint. That's more than you can say for a factory man; his bits and pieces scatter, grow wheels, disintegrate, change colour, join up in new forms which he doesn't know anything about. In short, he doesn't know what he's done, to whom.

A city commissioner's decision to switch from the brown paint that lasts two years to a silver paint that lasts eight years is motivated by the consideration that, instead of hiring a four-man team that gets the bridge painted every two years, they can economize by hiring one man to paint it in eight years. Albert wins the job, disregarding his family's hopes for his future. He marries a working-class girl, but gradually prefers to spend more and more extra hours on the bridge, far above the nagging wife and crying baby.

In his second year of painting—"my future traced in brown, my past measured in silver"—Albert is dismayed by a new presence on the girders with him. Fraser climbs up several times, always intending to commit suicide as a means of escape from the noise, chaos, and constant expansion of people and things in modern life. From the bridge's height, however, that disorder takes on the safe appearance of small, functional "dots and bricks, giving out a gentle hum." Albert complains to his employer about Fraser, but is told that all will be resolved on the following day, when 1,800 painters report to work to finish painting the entire bridge. Even though Albert is ahead of schedule, the rest of the bridge is overdue for its painting and is rusting badly.

On the girders the next day. Albert and Fraser see and hear the approach of 1,800 men, whistling "Colonel Bogey" as they march to the bridge. Unfortunately, the army of painters had not been instructed to break step as they moved onto the bridge. The pressures that build and tremble throughout the structure until the rivets pop are a metaphor for Fraser's view of a society filling out like a balloon, about to go bang. The bridge collapses.

Albert and Fraser are clones of Moon and Boot. Clive James (in "Count Zero Splits the Infinite," *Encounter*, November 1975) believes that Albert represents Stoppard as artist, with his detached perspective on life, and that Fraser is like Stoppard the man, who lives down among the chaos but periodically detaches himself. Fraser's mounting despair forces him to climb the bridge, where he loses his despair and descends to earth, where he again despairs—a cycle of reactions that parallels endless cycles of painting the bridge. It is a variation on Stoppard's habit of playing intellectual leapfrog with himself.

Similarities between *Albert's Bridge* and *Jumpers* and *Lord Malquist and Mr Moon* are readily apparent. Unlike Moon's end in the novel, however, Albert's death may be more easily accepted as a kind of cosmic justice—retribution for his having become so self-contained, so completely cut off from other people, including his wife and child. If Albert does represent the artist, there is an implicit warning to the artist not to become totally absorbed in his work or to become smugly satisfied with what he has accomplished. When Albert is only a temporary bridge-painter, he croons to himself songs of love, of the moon, and of faraway places. Two years later his only subject is himself; he substitutes "I" and me" for "you" in snatches of popular love songs. His last concerns before he goes down with the bridge (clearly echoing Rosencrantz and Guildenstern) are, "Was I so important?. . .What are they doing to my bridge? . . . To go to such lengths! I didn't do any harm! What did I have that they wanted?" The selfish delusion that one is contributing to a society from which one stands completely apart appears to be an even more unsound world view than the helpless passivity of Moon in *Lord Malquist and Mr Moon*.

The regimentation of "hundreds and hundreds of ordinary people—the overflow—all the fit men in the prime of life" to paint Albert's bridge is similar to the mindless subserviance of human beings to the clock and to inflexible schedules in *If You're Glad I'll Be Frank*. It is this very insistence upon an arbitrary kind of order in human activity that dehumanizes "the fit men in the prime of life" like Frank, who has so much love to offer, and that creates a sense of overwhelming chaos within the rigid pattern.

Frank is a bus driver who one day dials "T-I-M" on the telephone to verify the time and recognizes the voice of the speaking clock as that of his long-lost wife Gladys. He vows to find her and set her free, but is hampered by the bus schedule to which he must adhere. When he gains ninety seconds on his rounds, he pulls up at the telephone headquarters, leaving his busful of passengers momentarily stranded in traffic, while he tries to get a message about Gladys to the top man. An example of the obstacles he encounters is the Porter's admonition: "You can't park there after seven if the month's got an R in it or before nine if it hasn't except on Christmas and the Chairman's birthday should it fall in Lent."

Gladys receives Frank's hasty calls between bus runs, but she cannot answer him without losing the beat. The audience, however, gets to hear her resigned, philosophical interior monologue in counterpoint to her forced pronouncements on the hour, minute, and second. She longs for Frank to rescue her. In a final outburst of suppressed individuality, she contemplates sneezing or even whispering an obscenity on the telephone.

Frank forces his way into the presence of Lord Coot, the head bureaucrat in the telephone office, only to be told that the speaking clock is not Gladys but a machine. After Frank is ushered out, a secretary tells Lord Coot that the speaking clock is becoming hysterical. On the phone, Gladys sobs that she cannot go on, but Lord Coot tells her to think of the public and pull herself together. He gets her back on schedule and rings off, saying, "I'll check you again within the hour, as usual."

If You're Glad I'll be Frank may be favorably compared with the best plays of the Theater of the Absurd. Like Ionesco's *The Chairs*, N.F. Simpson's *One-Way Pendulum*, Beckett's *Krapp's Last Tape*, or Adamov's

Ping-Pong, it draws attention, but offers no solution, to
the problem of loss of human values in a world of pro-
liferating objects. The genuine comedy it extracts from
the clockwork regulation of modern life is balanced by a
tragic sense of futility at the end. The sequences in the
Telephone Services office parody bureaucratic agencies
that have lost sight of their original purpose to serve
human beings and that now function mechanistically,
manifesting an inflated degree of self-importance.
There is an absurd factor here that is more pointed than
in the city commission's meetings in *Albert's Bridge:*
the telephone-office bureaucrats are themselves the
slaves of timetables beyond their control. Although
Frank and Gladys are forced to function as
mechanisms, they display a few more touches of individuality than do many characters in Stoppard's plays.
Frank, at least, with his fighting spirit, resists designa-
tion as a Boot or a Moon.

Stoppard turned down invitations to write screenplays for several years before he finally succumbed to
it. He had hesitated partially out of fear that he would
be unable to protect his work, since in the theatre,
according to Stoppard, even under optimum conditions, the writer ends up with only about seventy per-
cent of what he meant—and working conditions were
bound to be worse in film. He explained: "A play is
something which happens behind closed doors between consenting adults; and a film is a kind of three-
ring circus, and the director is the elephant act, and the
writer is a sort of clod who comes on afterwards and
cleans up the mess."[13] His first venture into the world
of film was *The Engagement* (1970), a fifty-minute film
for television directed by a friend, Paul Joyce, for NBC
Television.

By 1972 Stoppard was saying that he would "like to
write a spy film or a Western," but he suspected that
even if he did write them, the films would not get

made, "because they'll find them 'too wordy.' "[14]
Stoppard's first script to be brought to movie theaters
was not a spy film or a Western, but "an intelligent film
about intelligent people."[15] This was a rewriting of
Thomas Wiseman's screenplay for his novel *The
Romantic Englishwoman*, which Stoppard did as a favor
for director Joseph Losey in 1975. Although the film
was largely neglected by the public, Stoppard's contribution was well received by reviewers:

Tom Stoppard wrote the adaptation of the Thomas Wiseman
novel, and his savagely witty dialogue enriches this comedy
of manners about a wealthy British suburban couple and the
German gigolo who disrupts their marriage. The verbal
polish of Stoppard's writing complements the elegant visual
style that Losey has achieved with the aid of cinematographer
Gerry Fisher and production designer Richard MacDonald.[16]

Verbal polish is also a distinctive feature of
Despair, a film directed by Rainer Werner Fassbinder,
for which Stoppard wrote the screenplay based upon
the novel of the same name by Vladimir Nabokov.
Stoppard was the perfect writer to transfer Nabokov's
verbal intricacies to the screen, in conjunction with
Fassbinder's baroque visual style. It is also worth not-
ing that exile is a recurrent Stoppardian theme,
perhaps because England and English were foreign to
him in his childhood. (According to T.E. Kalem,
"*Rosencrantz and Guildenstern Are Dead* is exile
through ignorance. The two mini-heroes do not understand Hamlet or Elsinore. *Jumpers* is exile from God.
No one can clearly divine his purposes or verify his
existence. *Travesties* is exile by intent, a rebellion
against social traditions and aesthetic norms."[17])
Despair explores the theme of exile in that its protagonist Hermann Hermann is a Russian émigré living
in Berlin, a foreign culture to which he has never completely adapted.

Stoppard has also done translation/adaptations of
three plays. In keeping with his quest for variety of
experience, each is from a different language. Slawomir
Mrozek's *Tango* was first translated from the Polish by
Nicholas Bethell, then adapted by Stoppard for production at the Aldwych Theatre in 1966. In 1973 he pre-
pared an English version of Federico García Lorca's
The House of Bernarda Alba for the Greenwich
Theatre. Since Stoppard knows no Spanish at all, he
worked from two literal translations. One of them,
done especially for his use by Bristol University student Katie Kendall, included notes and suggestions.
For example, she translated one sentence, "I wish the
awful pain of a nail would pierce her in the eyes," and
noted that reference to the crucifixion would be understood in the original. Stoppard's version was: "I wish
her the pain of Christ's nails hammered into her
eyeballs." His interpolation of the word "hammered"
was intended to prevent confusion of "nails" with
"fingernails."[18]

"For someone like me who enjoys writing dialogue
but has a terrible time writing plays, adaptation is joy
time," Stoppard has said. "It's a craftsman's job. . . .
You go around with a bag of tools doing jobs between
personal plays."[19] The main problem he has found with
translation is that "the more free you get the more
natural it sounds, the more literal the less natural.
These two lines have to come to some sort of a deal.
You have to find out where to cross the freedom line,
where the fidelity line."[20]

Stoppard was remarkably faithful to both the letter
and the spirit of Arthur Schnitzler's *Das Weite Land* in
the English version that Stoppard called *The Undiscovered Country*. Although others have translated the
title as *Distant Country* or *Vast Domain*, Stoppard's
choice is probably an allusion to a line from Hamlet's
"to be or not to be" soliloquy: "The undiscovered coun-

try from whose bourn no traveller returns." Working closely with a German-speaking student, he made minor cuts in the lengthy text, eliminated the walk-on character of Dr Meyer, and rendered individual lines with sparkling economy. Opening at the National Theatre on June 20, 1979, Stoppard's version was the English premiere of the 1911 play about the idyllic decadence of a Viennese social set that changes partners in adultery as casually as it does on the tennis court. The metaphor of the game, one of Stoppard's own favorite devices, must have appealed strongly to him, although he says that the choice of script was accidental:

While rehearsing *Night and Day* in a church hall in Chelsea, I saw a copy of a literal translation of *Undiscovered Country* on Peter Wood's table. I was just being nosy. They had asked somebody to adapt, but he pulled out. My interest was partly because Peter Wood would direct it and John Wood would act in it. Once I read the play, I agreed with Peter. It was remarkable, a play completely unknown in England, and worthy to stand with Ibsen and English contemporaries.[21]

A few examples from *The Undiscovered Country* will illustrate Stoppard's artistry as a translator/adapter. At the beginning of the play, there is talk of a funeral, at which tiresome speeches were made while mourners stood in a light rain. Hofreiter tells his wife that it was just as well she didn't go, because of—literally translated—"the pontifications . . . and the weather involved in it." Stoppard brilliantly and succinctly renders this: "between the drizzle and the drivel. . . ." In Act 3, the poet Rhon's wife returns from a mountain-climbing expedition, on which she spent her time playing dominoes:

> FRAU RHON: Are you cross with me? I won.
> RHON: Well, it's better than trying to climb the scenery anyway.

In another conversation, Rhon asks the fatuous young
Paul Kreindel about a play he had seen. A literal translation might be:

> RHON: What was being presented then?
> PAUL: Forgive me, but on that score I could hardly get
> excited, so to speak.
> RHON: For those people one pours out one's heart's
> blood.

Stoppard's original manuscript read:

> RHON: What was the play?
> PAUL: Frankly, I never noticed.
> RHON: One pours out one's life's blood for people like
> that.[22]

In the course of rehearsals, however, Paul's line was
elaborated as follows: "I never really noticed . . . Lots
of Frenchmen in wigs. I think it rhymed."[23]

"Through the efforts of Mr Stoppard and the National Theatre," Mel Gussow wrote in the *New York
Times* (July 15, 1979), *Undiscovered Country* "earns a
place in the international repertory." The question
posed by the title of a scholarly article on Stoppard,
"Serious Artist or Siren?"[24] may be favorably answered
in consideration of efforts such as this translation. It is a
sign of Stoppard's seriousness of purpose that he does
spend time refreshing his own creative drive at the well
of a master dramatist's work, and that these respectfully
executed projects do make the original newly accessible to a wide contemporary public.

6

Same Game, New Rules: Politics in Art

As a playwright who emerged in the turbulent 1960s, the decade of student protests and political unrest at all levels of society, Tom Stoppard has long been under pressure to write "political plays." The interviewer for *Theatre Quarterly* (May–June 1974), for example, questioned Stoppard repeatedly about his reluctance to write plays that grapple with current issues. Stoppard's responses to those questions expressed a basic philosophy about the place of the artist in society. He has not deviated in essence from that philosophy. However, four of his most recent plays—*Professional Foul, Every Good Boy Deserves Favour, Night and Day,* and *Cahoot's Macbeth*—demonstrate commitment to particular social and political views. It will be interesting to see whether this new willingness to integrate political thought with art indicates a major change of direction for his work.

"I'm not impressed by art *because* it's political," Stoppard told the *Theatre Quarterly* interviewer. "I believe in art being good art or bad art, not relevant art or irrelevant art." He is under no delusion that a work of art can change the course of governments or even affect the outcome of a single specific issue in the short term. "If you are angered or disgusted by a particular injustice or immorality, and you want to do something about it, *now, at once,* then you can hardly do worse than

write a play about it. That's what art is bad at." Just
because a work of art cannot do the short-term job that
a good journalistic piece can do, however, this does not
mean that art is unimportant in a sociopolitical sense,
or that it might as well be frivolous. What art is best at
is contributing to a long-term "universal perception."
Art "provides the moral matrix, the moral sensibility,
from which we make our judgments about the world."[1]

According to Stoppard, all judgments about the
world should be made on a moral basis. Political acts
and regimes should be set up against "a moral standard,
a consistent idea of what constitutes good and bad in
the way human beings treat each other regardless of
class, colour, or ideology," he said in 1974, "and at least
my poor professor in *Jumpers* got *that* right."[2] In 1979
he was still expressing himself in much the same vein:

I try to be consistent about moral behavior. Let other people
hang labels. It's a tactical distortion to label certain attitudes
right or left. I'm a conservative with a small c. I'm a conservative in politics, literature, education, and theater. My main
objection is to ideology and dogma—Holy Writ for
adherents.[3]

Elsewhere, Stoppard has defined himself as a supporter of "Western, liberal democracy, favoring an intellectual élite and a progressive middle class and based on a
moral order derived from Christian absolutes."[4]

Stoppard's sense of moral order is outraged by total-
itarianism under whatever ideological label a regime
chooses to disguise itself, be it Marxism, Leninism, or
fascism. This moral outrage at totalitarian violations of
human rights is the underlying thesis of his four "plays
of commitment." Explaining his political views to Kenneth Tynan, Stoppard said,

I don't lose any sleep if a policeman in Durham beats somebody up, because I know it's an exceptional case. It's a sheer
perversion of speech to describe the society I live in as one

that inflicts violence on the underprivileged. What worries
me is not the bourgeois exception but the totalitarian norm.
Of all the systems that are on offer, the one I don't want is the
one that denies freedom of expression—no matter what its
allegedly redeeming virtues may be. The only thing that
would make me leave England would be control over free
speech.[5]

Stoppard has long been a member of the
worldwide human rights organization, Amnesty International, and of its subsidiary Committee Against
Psychiatric Abuse (CAPA) which was created in Geneva
in 1975. He has also been an admirer of Czech playwright Václav Havel ever since he came across Havel's
plays in 1967. Stoppard feels a strong affinity for the
work of his Czech counterpart, only nine months older
than he, who shares his playfulness with language and
his oblique treatment of reality to gain a new perspective on the truth.

Havel had established himself as a playwright during Alexander Dubček's "thaw" in Czech socialism,
which was ended by the Soviet invasion of Czechoslovakia in August 1968 and its imposition of the neo-
Stalinist dictatorship of Gustav Husák. Havel's plays
have been banned from production in Czechoslovakia
since 1969. Although the charges against him were no
more specific than that his work gave a distorted picture of Czechoslovakian life, Havel was subjected to
various forms of harassment.

In January 1977, Havel and others organized a
human rights movement in Czechoslovakia. Their man-
ifesto, Charter 77, signed by 241 people, pointed out
that the Czechs had been deprived of freedom of
speech and worship and of the rights to privacy and due
process that had been guaranteed by the International
Covenants on Human Rights confirmed in Helsinki in
1975. For this, Havel was arrested and imprisoned for
four months. By June 1977, despite government perse-

cution of the original signers, there was a total of 750 names on the document. In 1979 it was estimated that over 2,000 Czechs had signed Charter 77,[6] while thousands of sympathizers refrain from doing so only because they fear reprisals against their children.[7]

Stoppard traveled to Czechoslovakia in June 1977 and spent five or six hours visiting with Havel. (Havel was jailed again in May 1979, along with several other dissident academics and intellectuals, and six months later he was sentenced to four and a half years in prison, on charges of slander and subversion against the state.) Stoppard was profoundly disturbed by events in Czechoslovakia, as well as by what he learned in meetings with Soviet dissidents on a trip to Moscow and Leningrad, on which he reported in an article, "The Face at the Window," in *The Sunday Times* (London, February 27, 1977, p. 33). Thus, when Mark Shivas of BBC Television expressed interest in producing whatever Stoppard had to offer, Stoppard was ready to write a play on the subject of human rights and to take advantage of the television medium to expose the problem to a mass audience. The result was *Professional Foul*, which was first broadcast on September 21, 1977. Stoppard has contributed all of his proceeds from that production to Amnesty International.

Professional Foul combines a suspenseful story with a serious examination of questions of human rights, individual rights, and collective or "state" ethics. Sprinkled less liberally (and less self-indulgently) than usual is a nonetheless delightful array of familiar Stoppardian devices: wordplay, qui pro quos, visual jokes, and reversals of expectations. To use academic intellectuals as the major figures in a ninety-minute television drama is unusual enough, but *Professional Foul* also contains some of the most subtle characterization in Stoppard's entire canon. (With reference to Stoppard's handling of this play and *Jumpers*, one philosophy professor is reported to have said: "He's very good. Perhaps not quite so good at philosophy itself but terribly good at philosophers—he gets them beautifully."[8])

Professsional Foul's appeal is flawed only by a few long stretches of George Moore-like theoretical discourse that challenge the attentiveness of the mass audience. Possibly this was a reason for balancing the Colloquium Philosophicum in Prague with something more down-to-earth—a World Cup qualifying soccer match played there between Czechoslovakia and England. This event occurring in the background to the main action provides material for several clever misinterpretations based upon overlapping political, philosophical, and sports vocabularies.

Three British professors of philosophy are introduced in a scene set on a passenger jet en route to Prague, where they are to present papers at a colloquium. Anderson, a fiftyish, fastidious type, who specializes in ethics, has the most firmly established academic position and reputation of the group. He betrays a certain prudishness when he is caught looking at a sleeping seatmate's sex magazine. His reserved manner in conversation creates the early impression that he is condescending and unsympathetic. The somewhat younger McKendrick is a specialist in "the philosophical assumptions of social science." He is personable and friendly, but there is a suggestion of the hypocrite in his overt enjoyment of "western decadence" (jazz and sex) despite his avowed Marxist leanings. Idealistic young Chetwyn, whose field is the history of philosophy, has been in the news lately with his letters to *The Times* about persecuted professors in Czechslovakia. McKendrick is surprised that the Czechs even gave Chetwyn a visa. The understated games of name-dropping and one-upmanship in this scene start the play on a note of lively humor.

In the hotel lobby, Anderson points out two young men named Crisp and Broadbent. McKendrick pretends to have heard of their work in philosophy, especially when Anderson mentions that Crisp is "left-wing." Only after several more amusing muddles does McKendrick later learn that they are the English soccer team.

Anderson is visited in his room by Pavel Hollar, who had been his student in England ten years earlier, before the 1968 Soviet crackdown in Czechoslovakia. Although he had been a brilliant student, Hollar's present job is cleaning bus-station lavatories. This reflects the situation Stoppard described in his article, "Prague: The Story of the Chartists," (*New York Review of Books*, August 4, 1977, p. 15):

The events of 1977 are in direct line with a process which since 1968/1969 has turned Czechoslovakia into a weird, upside-down country where you can find boilers stoked by economists, streets swept by men reading Henry James in English; where filing clerks rise early to write articles for learned journals abroad, and third-rate time-servers are chauffeured around in black, bulbous chrome-trimmed Tatra 603s straight out of a Fifties' spy film; where millions of crowns per month are spent on maintaining little cordons of policemen and vehicles to disarm a handful of dangerous men whose only weapon is free conversation.

Out of hearing of the hotel-room "bug," Hollar asks Anderson to smuggle the doctoral thesis he has written back to England. Anderson refuses, on the grounds that it would be unethical, since he has come to Czechoslovakia by invitation, as a guest of the government. Fearing that he may be searched on the way home from contact with a foreigner, Hollar asks Anderson to keep the thesis overnight and to bring it to his apartment the next day. Anderson agrees.

In a colloquium session the following morning, an American philosopher speaks on the logic of language. But the examples he uses defy all logic for the harried simultaneous translators. In the audience Anderson whispers to McKendrick that he is going to duck out and go to the soccer match. Since this means he will miss McKendrick's speech, McKendrick gives Anderson a copy of his paper.

On his way to the game by taxi, Anderson stops at Hollar's apartment to return Hollar's thesis, but he finds the building in an uproar. Although the dialogue in this scene is in Czech, it eventually becomes clear that Hollar was arrested the night before, that men have been searching the apartment continuously for the past twenty hours, and that Mrs Hollar chooses Anderson as the witness she is entitled to have during a search. Anderson is detained, but allowed to listen to the game on the radio.

An official finally arrives who speaks English. He tells Anderson that Hollar is charged with dealing in black-market currency. The fact that this is a lie is underscored by the radio announcement of a penalty called against the Czechs in the soccer match—a professional foul. The official threatens to search Anderson's briefcase, but Anderson forestalls this by surrendering McKendrick's paper as the harmless item of philosophical interest that he was going to deliver to Hollar. One of the searchers displays a bundle of American dollars purportedly found under the floorboards. Anderson is allowed to leave, too late for the game.

Back at the hotel, Anderson listens to Grayson, the sports reporter in the room adjoining his, call in his story to England; ("There'll be Czechs bouncing in the streets of Prague tonight as bankruptcy stares English football in the face . . . "). But Anderson's mind is no longer on the game that he had so much wanted to see. He goes to dinner, and, in a theoretical discussion with other philosophers, McKendrick refutes one of Anderson's points, saying, "So you end up using a moral principle as your excuse for acting against a moral interest." Unwittingly, McKendrick has pointed out to Anderson the truth about his refusal to help Hollar. Perhaps it is at this point that Anderson's change of heart occurs. When he glimpses Mrs Hollar, he follows her out quickly.

The most poignant scene in the play, the one that fully overwhelms Anderson with the awful truth about life under a totalitarian regime, takes place in a park at night. There, he converses with Mrs Hollar through her young son Sacha, who translates for them. Sacha tells Anderson that his father's imprisonment on trumped-up currency charges is really because he had signed Charter 77. He also warns that Anderson will undoubtedly be searched at the airport when he leaves. Sacha says he will send a philosopher-friend of his father's to the colloquium to pick up Hollar's thesis. Anderson promises to do what he can in England to get Hollar released from prison. Mrs Hollar and Sacha walk away into the dark.

Returning to the hotel, Anderson finds a small party going on in Grayson's room. McKendrick is drunk and behaving nastily, directing a stream of insults at the English soccer players. The reversal of empathic responses is complete: McKendrick has become thoroughly unsympathetic, while Anderson, who helps him to his room, has grown in stature. Anderson then borrows Grayson's typewriter for the night.

The next morning Anderson begins his scheduled speech to the colloquium by announcing that he will discuss "the conflict between the rights of individuals and the rights of the community." The chairman interrupts him, since this is a departure from Anderson's official paper, of which he and the simultaneous translators have copies. Anderson calmly responds by speaking more slowly for the translators. The chairman leaves the stage. There is a cut to Anderson's room, where plainclothes policemen are conducting a careful search. In the congress hall, Anderson continues to speak about the discrepancy between ethics and logic in totalitarian systems, until the proceedings are cut short by a fire-alarm bell.

At the airport the three philosophers departing for England are searched simultaneously at three different baggage-check stations. Anderson and Chetwyn are searched with a thoroughness that includes, for example, opening a cellophane-wrapped box of chocolates. Anderson looks anxious when a zippered sidepocket of his briefcase is opened. The customs official extracts from it, not Hollar's thesis, but a sex magazine that McKendrick had given the embarrassed Anderson. Chetwyn is detained upon discovery of some letters to Amnesty International inside a laundered shirt. McKendrick is searched only perfunctorily.

On the plane Anderson confesses to McKendrick that he had reversed one of his own principles and taken advantage of McKendrick's drunkenness of the previous night to place in his briefcase a thesis, that is "apparently rather slanderous from the state's point of view." McKendrick trembles with rage at having been used as an unknowing smuggler. He accuses Anderson of "not quite playing the game." Anderson replies, "You could be right. Ethics is a very complicated business. That's why they have these congresses."

Much of the suspense created in *Professional Foul* is based on character. After a certain point in the action, one does not doubt that Anderson will try to get Hollar's thesis out, even though no moment of decision is shown. The airport search is a gripping dramatic exploitation of the trust we have come to place in Anderson's character. The discovery of the sex magazine provides a good excuse for nervous laughter, but Stoppard must have intended the running joke to seem trivial now, in the light of all else we have seen. It actually serves to build tension toward the revelation of how Anderson used McKendrick. Even if the audience is not equipped to judge Anderson's actions ethically or philosophically, it accepts the denouement because Anderson has lost his rigidity and been willing to learn from experience, whereas McKendrick has seen and learned little.

In *Professional Foul* Stoppard performed his usual marriage of comic invention and serious idea content, but he added a new ingredient: moments of tragic poignancy. The skill with which these elements are blended is matched in Stoppard's canon only by *Every Good Boy Deserves Favour*, which premiered three months earlier. *Every Good Boy Deserves Favour* is an admirable experiment in theatre, "A Piece for Actors and Orchestra," but it is less satisfying as entertainment than *Professional Foul*, since the story is thin and its suspense is dissipated by the orchestral interpolations. In performance, the mere presence on stage of a full-sized live symphony orchestra conjures up a monumentality that the text, for all its admirable qualities, cannot match.

The genesis of *Every Good Boy Deserves Favour* is recounted in Tom Stoppard's program notes for the production and in notes by André Previn for the RCA recording of the original London production. In 1974, Previn invited Stoppard to write something which could be performed by actors in collaboration with a live orchestra on stage. Previn would then compose music for the orchestra to play between passages of dialogue. Stoppard was intrigued because "invitations don't come much rarer than that."

Stoppard's first idea was to write a play about a millionaire fruit-canner who owns a symphony or-

chestra that plays for him on command, night or day. At
some point in the creative process, Stoppard realized
that the orchestra need not be real; it could be a
figment of a madman's imagination. And if the orchestra were imaginary, the man no longer needed to
be a millionaire. Since Stoppard had played the
triangle in kindergarten, he decided to write about
a lunatic triangle-player who thinks he is backed up
by an orchestra. But still Stoppard had no idea for the
plot.

Meanwhile, Stoppard was going ahead with research on dissidents in Soviet-bloc countries, preparatory to writing *Professional Foul*. In 1976 he met Victor
Fainberg, who had been exiled from the USSR after
five years in Soviet prison-hospitals for his 1968 protest against the invasion of Czechoslovakia. Fainberg
wrote about an experience that many others had reported, being diagnosed as "insane" for speaking out
against political abuses. ("Your opinions are your symp-
toms," says the doctor in Stoppard's play.) At last Stoppard knew that his play would be about a political prisoner sharing a cell in an asylum with the lunatic
triangle-player.

Both men are named Alexander Ivanov, and, according to the logic of Soviet bureaucracy, this justifies
their being confined together. For purposes of clarity,
Stoppard calls the political prisoner Alex, and the
genuine mental patient Ivanov. Their cell with two
beds is a small platform down center in front of the
conductor. Two other acting areas share the stage with
the orchestra: the Doctor's office is behind the brasses,
and a schoolroom is behind the violins.

The audience laughs even before any dialogue is
spoken, for the entire orchestra silently mimes playing
the music that Ivanov seems to hear as he stands in his
cell. Gradually the orchestra becomes audible to the
audience, as it actually begins to play the music Ivanov
hears in his imagination. Alex knows about his

cellmate's delusion and tries hard not cough until Ivanov stops striking his triangle and sits down—a sign to Alex that Ivanov's "orchestra" has finished. Ivanov apologizes for the poor performance of the cellos, and Alexander replies cautiously, "I'm not really a judge of music." There follows an extraordinary cascade of musicoverbal wit: references to plucky harpists, a Jew's harp that has applied for a visa, French whores and gigolos (horns and piccolos), and a trombone thrown to a dog.

Like *Professional Foul, Every Good Boy Deserves Favour* derives much of its poignancy from the simple wisdom of a child in opposition to the monolithic system that distorts logic to protect itself. Again, the boy is called Sacha and he is the son of the imprisoned dissident. He resists regimentation ("I don't want to be in the orchestra"), and he creates his own definitions in geometry ("A plane area bordered by high walls is a prison not a hospital"). Sacha is thus the reference for the play's title, which is also the English mnemonic device for EGBDF on the piano.

The Doctor in the asylum is an incompetent functionary whose main interest is playing the violin in a real orchestra. His movements are mimicked by a frivolous oboe. In a session with Ivanov, he says, "We cannot make progress until we agree that there is no orchestra," and Ivanov replies, "Or until we agree that there is." Ivanov willingly parrots the Doctor's declarations that "there is no orchestra," but then asks one favor: "Will you stop them playing?"

Alex's "affliction" and his reasons for refusing to recant are expressed in his scenes with the Doctor and in a monologue recounting actual repressive measures taken against Russian dissidents, with letters of the alphabet used in place of names like Fainberg and Bukhovsky. In a touching scene between father and son, Sacha begs Alex to admit he was insane for saying that sane people are put in mental hospitals.

SACHA: Tell them lies. Tell them they've cured you. Tell them you're grateful

ALEX. How can that be right?

SACHA: If they're wicked how can it be wrong?

ALEX: It helps them to go on being wicked. It helps people to think that perhaps they're not so wicked after all.

The impasse is resolved when a pompous Soviet official makes a mock-heroic entrance and interrogates the two inmates, with comic grandeur, brushing aside the obsequious Doctor. When he barks "Alexander Ivanov," both men stand up. He asks Ivanov if he thinks a Soviet doctor would put a sane man into a lunatic asylum, and he asks Alex if he hears any music. Both men reply negatively and are ordered released.

The conformists—Sacha's teacher, the Doctor, and Ivanov—take places in the orchestra. Alex leaves the cell to follow Sacha, who sings that "everything can be all right," an ending that might be interpreted as either optimistic or pessimistic. When it was staged at the Metropolitan Opera House in New York in 1979, the ending was highly theatrical, with an upstage center exit in a shaft of light. Intellectually, however, something was lacking. A dissident espousing Alex's principles could not stand quietly by, while another assumed his identity and affirmed a lie. On the other hand, the Doctor, at least, was witness to Alex's integrity, and there is a feeling that an individual has triumphed over the system. One critic said, "The surprise ending will please those who believe that if Soviet communism is ever toppled it will be by neither dissidence nor art but by its own bureaucratic confusion."[9] Another reviewer was bothered by the ending for other reasons:

The resolution is complicated by the relativism between insanity and the rational mind, for the audience begins to question the reality of the happy ending. After all, the madman *imagines* his orchestra, yet there the orchestra is, 80-strong, on the platform before the viewers' eyes. Who then is insane—the artist with music within him, or the state which dictates the only acceptable thoughts a man may carry inside his *head*?[10]

It is true that the use of an orchestra as a metaphor for an orchestrated society is somewhat disconcerting to artists. Mel Gussow summed up that reservation in his review:

The comment—the dissident as the discordant note in society—works for the theatrical part of the evening, but what does "Every Good Boy" say about the society of the orchestra? What if all the triangles, piccolos, cellos, and kettle drums went blissfully in their own direction without benefit of score or conductor? The result would not be dissidence or dissonance but cacaphony. Perhaps covertly " Every Good Boy" is intended as a piece of music criticism.[11]

In general, critics raised few objections to Stoppard's device, although filmmaker Federico Fellini was lambasted for his use of the same metaphor in *Orchestra Rehearsal,* which was, coincidentally, released in August 1979, and which also runs about seventy minutes. The distinction may be that Stoppard's metaphor is merely a conceit, a flight of fancy, whereas Fellini forced it heavy-handedly into the realm of agitprop.

Stoppard's scrupulous avoidance of propaganda techniques—that is, his characteristically balanced presentation of both sides of a given topic equally persuasively—caused some confused reactions to *Night and Day.* Robert Berkvist reported in the *New York Times* (November 25, 1979) that some of the audience saw the play as "a scathing attack on journalism." Stoppard's own position, as one might expect of a former newspaper reporter, was quite the opposite: "I'm a lover of and apologist for journalism. The play actually is saying that the aspects of journalism which one might well disapprove of are the price we pay for the part that matters, and that the part that matters is absolutely vital."

Night and Day is perhaps Stoppard's most conventional play. It is, in Stoppard's own words, "one of those beginning, middle, and end plays with one set and eight characters, including a woman who's falling for somebody." It came about as a merging of several impulses. He wanted to demonstrate that he "could actually write a story-telling number, one in which people don't suddenly jump through hoops and recite a poem," and that he could write "a really good part for a woman." He also wanted to write a love story, and he wanted to write a play about journalism.[12] *Night and Day* is certainly about journalism and has a "love story," as the term is understood nowadays—not a romance, but an incident of physical attraction between strangers.

The woman who dominates the play like a calm spot in the center of a storm is Ruth Carson, wife of a British mine owner in a ficticious African country that was formerly a British colony. Ruth's interactions with her husband, with her eight-year-old son Alastair, with her one-night-stand lover Richard Wagner, and with her fantasy-lover Jacob Milne are shallow and unsatisfying; each seems to regard her as serving a largely decorative function. Yet she is not a superficial character. Like Ibsen's Hedda Gabler, she is a woman of unrealized potential trapped by the limiting horizons of provincial life and by an unfulfilling marriage; but, instead of following Hedda Gabler's path of destruction, Ruth turns inward and talks to herself. ("I talk to myself in the middle of a conversation. In fact I talk to myself in the middle of an *imaginary* conversation, which is itself a refuge from some other conversation altogether, frequently imaginary.")

Night and Day departs from conventional realism in that the audience is allowed to hear Ruth's thoughts, which are spoken aloud, sometimes contradicting or interrupted by her actual dialogue with other characters. The technique is not wholly experimental, since

Eugene O'Neill used it for several characters in *Strange Interlude* as early as 1928. Nor is it gratuitous, for it enhances Ruth's characterization as "still waters" that "run deep," and it permits the staging of a seduction that occurs only in the woman's imagination. What is less clear is the reason for Ruth's preoccupation with movies. Many of the references are so subtle as to be almost unnoticeable, but they add up: *Help* (the Beatles' movie), *Pygmalion* or *My Fair Lady*, *Elephant Walk*, *King Solomon's Mines*, "I'm in the wrong movie," "Watch yourself, Tallulah," and other lines clearly derived from unnamed gems of the silver screen. Ruth's role in this play offers interesting points of comparison with that of Elizabeth Taylor in *Elephant Walk*. Diana Rigg in the London production and Maggie Smith in New York both received overwhelming praise for their interpretations of the complex role.

The action takes place in the Carsons' large comfortable house in the fictitious country of Kambawe. Three journalists for the *Sunday Globe* converge upon the house, drawn by the telex Carson uses for business communications, which will allow them to scoop rival newspapers in getting out reports of recent unrest in Kambawe. The repressive dictatorship of British-educated President Mageeba is being challenged by a Soviet-supported rebellion led by Colonel Shimbu. The scenario is as familiar as today's news:

[Mageeba is] going to go in with air strikes and tanks and lose half of them in a week, and appeal to the free world about Russian interference. I also think that the British and the Americans will protest, and all the time they're protesting the Russians will be interfering the stuffing out of Mageeba's army, until Kambawe is about as independent as Lithuania, and *that* the British and Americans will protest.

Wagner and Guthrie are a veteran reporter-photographer journalistic team, but they have been outdone by a young free-lance reporter, Milne, who chanced to get an interview with Shimbu and sent it to the *Globe*. The rivalry that develops between Wagner and Milne is fueled by the fact that Wagner is a staunch union supporter, whereas young Milne recently gained a certain notoriety by refusing on principle to join a union strike at the small local newspaper in England where he worked until he decided to go to Africa on his own in search of bigger stories. When Milne uses Carson's telex to send a new story to the *Globe*, Wagner adds a message of his own, a protest against the employment of the nonunion Milne.

Wagner is eager at first to use Carson's pass to travel with Guthrie into territory held by Shimbu, to cover events there. When he learns from little Alastair that President Mageeba will visit the Carson home the next evening, he affects generosity in allowing Milne to go out instead. Since Milne has already contributed a story on Shimbu's activities, an interview with the equally elusive Mageeba would be an even bigger story.

In her brief conversation with Milne, Ruth is attracted by his idealism. Whereas Wagner sees the *Globe* as "a million packets of journalism manufactured every week by businessmen using journalists for their labor," to Milne it is "a free press, free expression—it's the last line of defense for all the other freedoms." Ruth had been deeply hurt by the press's sensational coverage of Carson's divorce from his first wife and subsequent marriage to her. She sums up her attitude: "The populace and the popular press. What a grubby symbiosis it is."

Milne's principles are firm: "Junk journalism is the evidence of a society that has got at least one thing right, that there should be nobody with the power to dictate where responsible journalism begins." And he says that "no matter how imperfect things are, if you've got a free press everything is correctable, and without it everything is concealable." Ruth responds: "I'm with you on the free press. It's the newspapers I can't stand."

The next day, while Milne is off in the jeep with Guthrie, Ruth fantasizes breaking down his high principles and seducing him, a reverie that is actually played on stage by the two characters. It is interrupted by Wagner, who has driven out to the house, uninvited, in hopes of seeing Mageeba.

Mageeba arrives with a toy machine gun as a gift for Alastair. Wagner tries to be ingratiating, but Mageeba takes a dislike to him. In the course of their discussion of journalism, Mageeba defines "a relatively free press" as "a free press which is edited by one of my relatives." Then he strikes Wagner on the head with his metal-knobbed cane.

Guthrie returns unexpectedly and announces that Milne is dead, shot by Mageeba's men, despite the supposed "cease-fire" and despite journalistic immunity. Delayed en route, they had risked going on after dark because "the *Globe* is a Sunday paper. If you miss it by an hour you've missed it by a week." Guthrie addresses a stream of obscenties at Mageeba, who exits declaring all-out war on Shimbu.

Carson warns Guthrie and Wagner to leave Kambawe immediately, since both have reason to fear Mageeba's wrath. Both men decide to stay, despite Ruth's protest that no story is worth dying for. As far as she can see, Milne died "for the women's page, and the crossword, and the racing results." Guthrie's response is Stoppard's own credo: "People do awful things to each other. But it's worse in places where everybody is kept in the dark. It really is. Information, in itself, about anything, is light. That's all you can say, really." (It is worth recalling that lack of information is precisely what saps the spirits of Rosencrantz and Guildenstern in Stoppard's play of eleven years earlier.)

The final irony in *Night and Day* is that Wagner's

exclusive interview with Mageeba was useless. A telex message notifies them that Wagner's protest of Milne's nonunion status caused a management-worker confrontation at the *Globe*, resulting in a weekend shutdown; there will be no issue of the *Globe* this week. Wagner then sends a report of Milne's death to the young man's former local newspaper. The play ends on the suggestion that Ruth, whose husband has left again on business, will repeat her casual infidelity with Wagner.

Night and Day brought mixed reactions from reviewers of both the London and New York productions, several of whom compared it to the work of George Bernard Shaw. Reservations about the play tended to be vague: "more garrulous than witty";[13] "odd moments of strain";[14] "The all-too-carefully crafted combination makes one uneasy";[15] "The author's most perplexing and, in so many respects, least satisfying work. . . . occasionally his talent is like some Jumbo jet coming in to land on the narrowest of fences."[16]

Whatever such objections are worth, one has only to compare any dialogue sequence or any character from *Night and Day* with a sample from *Rosencrantz and Guildenstern Are Dead* to see how well Stoppard's talent has matured in twelve years. If he is purging his writing of its self-consciously or self-indulgently clever aspects, he has not, it seems, renounced his obligation to Shakespeare. A reference to—or a phrase from—Shakespeare appears in almost every play, like a "signature," the way Alfred Hitchcock pops up in each of his own films. In *Night and Day*, Ruth gaily blurts out to Mageeba: "Well—uneasy lies the head that—" (from *King Henry IV, Part 2*, "Uneasy lies the head that wears a crown."). And why else would the much-discussed newspaper in the play be called the *Globe?*

Shakespeare was also a resource for *Cahoot's Macbeth*, the second half of the production that inaugurated the British American Repertory Company; (the first half of the bill, *Dogg's Hamlet*, is discussed in Chapter 5, along with a summary of BARC's aims). Stoppard has pointed out that *Dogg's Hamlet* can be produced without *Cahoot's Macbeth*, but that the latter "cannot be done unless you've seen the first one first." This is a pity, because the wit, thought, and entertainment values of *Cahoot's Macbeth* far outshine the tedious foolishness of the frame story in *Dogg's Hamlet*.

Stoppard conceived the premise of *Cahoot's Macbeth* after receiving a letter from Pavel Kohout, another dissident Czech playwright Stoppard had met on his 1977 visit to Prague. (Kohout's works are banned from performance and publication in Czechoslovakia, but his play *Poor Murderer* was produced on Broadway in 1976. It is about a young Russian actor confined to a mental institution since he went mad in the role of Hamlet.) In his letter to Stoppard, Kohout described his recent activity:

As you know, many Czech theatre people are not allowed to work in the theatre during these last years. As one of them who cannot live without theatre I was searching for a possibility to do theatre in spite of circumstances. Now I am glad to tell you that in a few days, after eight weeks of rehearsals—a Living-Room Theatre is opening with nothing smaller than *Macbeth*. What is L.R.T.? A call-group. Everybody, who wants to have Macbeth at home with two great and forbidden Czech actors, Pavel Landovsky and Vlasta Chramostova, can invite his friends and call us. Five people will come with one suitcase.[17]

Like Kohout's living-room *Macbeth*, the abridgement of *Macbeth* in Stoppard's play can be performed by as few as five actors. Stoppard omitted four characters used by Kohout (Donalbain, Wounded Captain, Macduff's Wife, and a second messenger), but otherwise the role distribution would be the same:

FIRST ACTOR: Macbeth
SECOND ACTOR: Duncan, Banquo, Macduff, First Murderer, First Messenger
THIRD ACTOR: Ross, Malcolm, Second Murderer, Third Witch
FIRST ACTRESS: Second Witch, Servant
SECOND ACTRESS: Lady Macbeth, Third Witch

There are three additional characters in *Cahoot's Macbeth*, who do not act in the play-within-the-play. These are the Hostess in whose apartment *Macbeth* is performed; the Inspector, who is not so different from his counterparts in *Jumpers* and *The Real Inspector Hound*; and Easy, who is this play's link with *Dogg's Hamlet*. The action takes place in the living room of a flat in an unnamed totalitarian country, but Stoppard insists that "Cahoot is not Kohout, and the necessarily over-truncated 'Macbeth' is not supposed to be a fair representation of Kohout's elegant seventy-five-minute version."

Cahoot's Macbeth begins with Macbeth's encounter with the three witches and proceeds briskly through the highlights of Shakespeare's text to the murder of Duncan. As soon as Macbeth reenters with the bloodstained daggers and says "I have done the deed. Didst thou not hear a noise?," a police siren is heard approaching the house. The knocking at the gate in *Macbeth* becomes the Inspector's knock at the door of the apartment. The Inspector interrupts the performance, interrogates the actors, addresses the "bug" in the ceiling, and tells the Hostess, "If you had any pride in your home you wouldn't take standing-room-only in your sitting-room lying down."

Finally the Inspector orders the actors to resume their performance while he watches and to give it their best, because, "If I walk out of this show I take it with me." This time the actors get as far as Macbeth's coronation, which the Inspector takes to be a "happy ending." Then he indulges in some ideological banter with the Hostess and performers. The lines are hilarious—some of the funniest Stoppard has ever written, but the undertone is heartbreaking. The Inspector warns the troupe not to repeat their performance: "The fact is, when you get a universal and timeless writer like Shakespeare, there's a strong feeling that he could be spitting in the eye of the beholder. . . . " This is, of course, precisely the troupe's intention, and Shakespeare's lines are amazingly apropos. Of numerous examples, one might cite this: "Bleed, bleed, poor country!" "It weeps, it bleeds, and each new day a gash is added to her wounds."

As soon as the Inspector leaves, the actors pick up where they left off in the play, but they are soon interrupted again. Easy, the truck driver from *Dogg's Hamlet*, parks his truck outside the apartment window and enters. Since Easy now speaks only Dogg's language (see Chapter 5), he is shunted aside while the play continues. During the banquet scene at which Banquo's ghost appears to Macbeth, Easy pops in and out of view coincidentally with Macbeth's vision. Finally, Easy gets the group's attention and, with the help of his phrase book, makes it clear that he has a truckload of wooden blocks, slabs, and cubes to deliver here.

Communication becomes easier as actors and audience begin picking up Dogg's language ("You don't learn it, you catch it"). Stoppard is implying that people can understand each other when they have a common interest, despite language barriers. He had proved this indirectly in several earlier plays. The opening dialogue in *Dirty Linen* between two M.P.s is all French and Latin catch phrases. *Travesties* opens with a multilingual scene and incorporates Russian dialogue sequences between Lenin and Nadya. A long sequence in *Professional Foul* is performed entirely in Czech.

Like *Cahoot's Macbeth*, *Dogg's Our Pet* and *Dogg's Hamlet* both make extensive use of Dogg's language. In every instance, the audience switches quickly to other sign-symbol systems (facial expression, gestures, inflection) for its understanding of what is going on. Enjoyment of these scenes is not impaired and is often enhanced.

The Inspector returns and becomes involved in spite of himself in unloading wood from the truck and building a step unit in the living room. Meanwhile, the performance resumes in Dogg's language. The passing of blocks of wood along a human chain from the truck and in through the window coincides with the scene in which Birnam Wood comes to Dunsinane. Macbeth's famous lines, "Tomorrow, and tomorrow, and tomorrow,/ Creeps in this petty pace from day to day/To the last syllable of recorded time . . ." becomes, in Dogg's language: "Dominoes, et dominoes, et dominoes,/Popsies historical axle-grease,/ Exacts bubbly fins crock lavendar. . . . " The Inspector takes a telephone call from the "bug" and says into the phone: "How the hell do I know? But if it's not free expression, I don't know what is!"

The step unit is built just in time for the crowning of Malcolm on it. But the Inspector keeps working. He calls for more and more slabs and begins raising a wall. The metaphor is brilliant: artists under a totalitarian regime are physically walled in, but their thoughts and creative imaginations find their own form of expression—if necessary, a whole new language. As an ending to a play, the metaphor sums up what is best in Stoppard's sense of theatricality—the neatness of the packaging, the mutual reinforcement of visual and verbal cues, and the provocation to thought that seems like entertainment. As a statement, the ending of *Cahoot's Macbeth* is both an admission of horrors that exist in the human condition and a paean to the irrepressible human spirit.

Notes

1. VISITOR PLAYING THE FIELD

1. Kenneth Tynan, "Profiles," *New Yorker* (December 19, 1977), p. 41.
2. Mark Amory, "The Joke's the Thing," *Sunday Times Magazine* (June 9, 1974), p. 65.
3. "Tom Stoppard," *Current Biography* (1974), p. 396.
4. Tom Stoppard, "Ambushes for the Audience: Towards a High Comedy of Ideas," *Theatre Quarterly* (May–July 1974), p. 3.
5. Tynan, p. 46.
6. Amory, p. 66.
7. Tynan, p. 51.
8. Mel Gussow, "Stoppard Refutes Himself, Endlessly," *New York Times* (April 26, 1972), p. 54.
9. Bruce Cook, "Tom Stoppard: The Man Behind the Plays," *Saturday Review* (January 1, 1977), p. 53.
10. Jon Bradshaw, "Tom Stoppard, Nonstop," *New York* (January 10, 1977), p. 50.
11. Stoppard, "Ambushes for the Audience," p. 4.
12. Stoppard, "The Definite Maybe," *Author* 78 (Spring 1967), p. 19.
13. Stoppard, "Ambushes for the Audience," p. 5.
14. Ibid.
15. Stoppard, "The Definite Maybe," p. 19.
16. "Playwright, Novelist," *New Yorker* (May 4, 1968), p. 41.
17. Amory, p. 67.
18. Stoppard, "Ambushes for the Audience," p. 6.
19. Tynan, p. 65.

20. Ibid., p. 57
21. Amory, p. 67.
22. Ibid.
23. Bradshaw, p. 48.
24. T.E. Kalem, "Ping-Pong Philosopher," *Time* (May 6, 1974), p. 85.
25. Giles Gordon, "Tom Stoppard," *Transatlantic Review* 29 (Summer 1968), p. 18.
26. Barry Norman, "Tom Stoppard and the Contentment of Insecurity," *The Times* (November 11, 1972), p. 11.
27. Tynan, pp. 80–82.
28. Ibid., p. 109.
29. Bradshaw, p. 50.
30. Gussow, p. 54.
31. Tynan, p. 65.
32. Ibid., p. 93.
33. Gussow, p. 54.
34. Ibid.

2.   HOME FREE: *Rosencrantz and Guildenstern Are Dead*

1. Harold Clurman, "Theatre," *The Nation* 221 (August 16, 1975), p. 123.
2. Tom Stoppard, *Rosencrantz and Guildenstern Are Dead* (New York: Grove Press, 1967), pp. 78–84.
3. Ruth M. Goldstein, "A Discussion Guide (Second Edition) for the Play *Rosencrantz and Guildenstern Are Dead* by Tom Stoppard" (New York: Grove Press), p. 3.
4. Stoppard, "Doers and Thinkers: Playwrights and Professors," *Times Literary Supplement* (October 13, 1972), p. 1219.
5. Giles Gordon, "Tom Stoppard," *Transatlantic Review* 29 (Summer 1968), p. 22.
6. Leonard Powlick, personal interview (June 18, 1979, New York City).
7. Martin Esslin, *The Theatre of the Absurd* (Garden City, New York: Doubleday, 1969).

8. Ronald Hayman, *Tom Stoppard* (London: Heinemann, 1978), p. 46.

9. Robert Brustein, "Waiting for Hamlet," in *The Third Theatre* (New York: Alfred A. Knopf, 1969), pp. 149–153.

10. Anthony Callen, "Stoppard's *Godot*," *New Theater Magazine* (Winter 1969), pp. 22–30.

11. Stoppard, "Something to Declare," *The Sunday Times* (London, February 25, 1968), p. 47.

12. Callen, p. 27.

13. Gordon, p. 23.

14. Luigi Pirandello, "Preface to *Six Characters in Search of an Author*" in *Naked Masks: Five Plays,* ed. by Eric Bentley (New York: E.P. Dutton, 1952), p. 367.

15. Keith Harper, "The Devious Road to Waterloo," *The Guardian* (April 12, 1967), p. 7.

16. Brustein, p. 151, and John Weightman, "Mini-Hamlets in Limbo," *Encounter* 29 (July 1967), p. 38.

17. Gordon, p. 20.

18. Kenneth Tynan, "Profiles," *New Yorker* (December 19, 1977), p. 109.

19. Tom Prideaux, " 'Who Are We?' 'I Don't Know'," *Life* 64 (February 9, 1968), p. 73.

20. Jon Bradshaw, "Tom Stoppard, Nonstop," *New York* (January 10, 1977), p. 50.

21. C.O. Gardner, "Correspondence: *Rosencrantz and Guildenstern Are Dead,*" *Theoria* 34 (1969), p. 83.

22. Robert Egan, "A Thin Beam of Light: The Purpose of Playing in *Rosencrantz and Guildenstern Are Dead,*" *Theatre Journal* (March 1979), pp. 59–69.

23. Mark Amory, "The Joke's the Thing," *Sunday Times Magazine* (June 9, 1974), p. 70.

3.   MAGISTER LUDI: *Jumpers* AND *Travesties*

1. Janet Watts, "Tom Stoppard," *The Guardian* (May 21, 1973), p. 12.

2. Tom Stoppard, "Doers and Thinkers," *Times Literary Supplement* (October 13, 1972), p. 1219.

3. Stoppard, "Ambushes for the Audience," *Theatre Quarterly* (May–June 1974), p. 7.

4. Stoppard, "Doers and Thinkers," p. 1219.

5. Stoppard, "Ambushes for the Audience," p. 13

6. Ibid., pp. 6–7.

7. Ibid., p. 16.

8. "Theatre: The Best of the Seventies," *Time* (January 7, 1980), p. 97.

9. Stoppard, *Jumpers* (New York: Grove Press, 1972), p. 48.

10. Philip Roberts, "Tom Stoppard: Serious Artist or Siren?," *Critical Quarterly* (Autumn 1978), p. 86.

11. John Weightman, 'A Metaphysical Comedy," *Encounter* (April 1972), p. 45.

12. Charles Marowitz, "Tom Stoppard—The Theatre's Intellectual P.T. Barnum," *New York Times* (October 19, 1975), II, p. 5.

13. Richard Ellmann, "The Zealots of Zurich," *Times Literary Supplement* (July 12, 1974), p. 744.

14. Marowitz, p. 5.

15. Ronald Hayman, *Tom Stoppard* (London: Heinemann, 1978), p. 3.

16. Marowitz, p. 5.

17. T.E. Kalem, "Dance of Words," *Time* (November 10, 1975), p. 75.

18. Marowitz, p. 1.

19. Kenneth Tynan, "Profiles," *New Yorker* (December 19, 1977), p. 107.

20. Marowitz, p. 5.

21. Douglass Watt, "A Dazzling Play and Star," *New York Daily News* (October 31, 1975).

22. Jack Kroll, "Stars over Zurich," *Newsweek* (November 10, 1975).

23. Mark Amory, "The Joke's the Thing," *Sunday Times Magazine* (June 9, 1974), p. 70.

24. He is larger-than-life, is called Tzara,
    Who rushes headlong once again. Peerless jokester!
    He stays in Switzerland because he is an artist.
    "We have only art!" were his words.

25. Hayman, p. 3.

26. Stoppard, "Something to Declare," *The Sunday Times* (February 25, 1968), p. 47.
27. Tynan, p. 101.
28. Allan Rodway, "Stripping Off," *London Magazine* (August–September 1976), p. 71.
29. Ibid., p. 72.
30. Stoppard, "But for the Middle Classes," review of *Enemies of Society* by Paul Johnson, *Times Literary Supplement* (June 3, 1977), p. 677.
31. Tynan, p. 107.
32. Kalem, p. 75.
33. Hayman, p. 10.
34. Ibid., p. 10.
35. Ibid., p. 11.
36. Ibid., p. 128.
37. Ibid., p. 12.

4.   NARRATIVE PROSE ON THE SIDELINES:
SHORT STORIES AND A NOVEL

1. Nathalie Sarraute in *L'Ere de Soupçon* (1956), cited by Bettina Knapp, "Nathalie Sarraute: A Theatre of Tropisms," *Performing Arts Journal* (Winter 1977), p. 15.
2. Ronald Hayman, *Tom Stoppard* (London: Heinemann, 1978), pp. 21–22.
3. Ibid., p. 23.
4. Kathleen Halton, "Tom Stoppard," *Vogue* (October 15, 1967), p. 112.

5.   BOOTS AND MOONS: SORT COMEDIES,
RADIO PLAYS, SCREENPLAYS, AND TRANSLATIONS

1. Kenneth Tynan, "Profiles," *New Yorker* (December 19, 1977), p. 57.
2. Tom Stoppard, "Ambushes for the Audience," *Theatre Quarterly* (May–June 1974), p. 17.
3. Ibid.
4. Ibid.

5. Tynan, p. 57.

6. Stoppard, "Something to Declare," *The Sunday Times* (February 25, 1968), p. 47.

7. Ronald Hayman, *Tom Stoppard* (London: Heinemann, 1978), pp. 14–15.

8. Stoppard, "Ambushes for the Audience," p. 5.

9. Ibid., p. 8.

10. Wendell V. Harris, *"After Magritte," The Explicator* 34 (January 1976).

11. Jon Bradshaw, "Tom Stoppard, Nonstop," *New York* (January 10, 1977), p. 51.

12. *Catalogue of an Exhibition of Paintings by René Magritte, 1898–1967, Arranged by the Arts Council at the Tate Gallery, 14 February to 30 March 1969.* Introduction by David Sylvester (London: The Arts Council, 1969), p. 28.

13. Stoppard, "I'm Not Keen on Experiments," *New York Times* (March 8, 1970), II, p. 17.

14. Jerry Tallmer, "Tom Stoppard Pops in on the Cast." *New York Post* (August 26, 1977), p. 15.

15. Vincent Canby, "The Romantic Englishwoman," *New York Times* (November 27, 1975), p. 46.

16. Stephen Farber, "A Neglected Film about Modern Marriage," *New York Times* (January 18, 1976), II, p. 13.

17. T.E. Kalem, "Dance of Words," *Time* (November 10, 1975), p. 75.

18. "Tom Stoppard: *The House of Bernarda Alba,"* *Plays and Players* (April 1973), p. 38.

19. Mel Gussow, "Stoppard's Intellectual Cartwheels Now with Music," *New York Times* (July 29, 1979), p. 22.

20. *Plays and Players,* p. 38.

21. Gussow, "Stoppard's Intellectual Cartwheels," p. 22.

22. Arthur Schnitzler, *The Undiscovered Country,* English version by Tom Stoppard. Manuscript dated April 1979, lent by the National Theatre, London.

23. Gussow, "Schnitzler's Vienna as Told to Stoppard," *New York Times* (July 15, 1979), p. 6.

24. Philip Roberts, "Tom Stoppard: Serious Artist or Siren?," *Critical Quarterly* (Autumn 1978).

6.   SAME GAME, NEW RULES: POLITICS IN ART

1. Tom Stoppard, "Ambushes for the Audience," *Theatre Quarterly* (May–June 1974), p. 14.
2. Ibid., p. 12.
3. Mel Gussow, "Stoppard's Intellectual Cartwheels Now With Music," *New York Times* (July 19, 1977), p. 22.
4. Kenneth Tynan, "Profiles," *New Yorker* (December 19, 1977), p. 86.
5. Ibid., p. 93.
6. Sue Masterman, "Signers of Human Rights Charter Face Trials, Imprisonment in Czechoslovakia," *Chronicle of Higher Education* (October 29, 1979), p. 5.
7. Stoppard, "Prague: The Story of the Chartists," *New York Review of Books* 24 (August 4, 1977), p. 14.
8. "Dons Wave Play On," *The Times Higher Education Supplement* (September 30, 1977), p. 5.
9. Peter Stothard, "Every Good Boy Deserves Favour," *Plays and Players* 24 (September 1977), p. 33.
10. Albert E. Kalson, "Theatre in Review," *Educational Theatre Journal* (December 1977), 562.
12. Robert Berkvist, "This Time, Stoppard Plays It (Almost) Straight," *New York Times* (November 25, 1979) II, pp. 1, 5.
13. Brendan Gill, "The Theatre," *New Yorker* (December 10, 1979), p. 113.
14. T.E. Kalem, "Theater," *Time* (November 27, 1978), p. 110.
15. Jack Kroll, "Oh, to be in England," *Newsweek* (November 27, 1978), p. 66.
16. Steve Grant, *"Night and Day," Plays and Players* 26 (January 1979), pp. 18–19.
17. Schuyler Livingston, "BARC!," *Theatre News* 11 (September–October 1979), p. 9.

Bibliography

Works by Tom Stoppard

Rosencrantz and Guildenstern Are Dead. New York: Grove Press, Inc., 1967.

Enter A Free Man. New York: Grove Press, Inc., 1972.

Jumpers. New York: Grove Press, Inc., 1972.

Lord Malquist and Mr Moon. New York: Grove Press, Inc., 1975.

The Real Inspector Hound and *After Magritte.* New York: Grove Press, Inc., 1975.

Travesties. New York: Grove Press, Inc., 1975.

Dirty Linen and *New-Found-Land.* New York: Grove Press, Inc., 1976.

Albert's Bridge and Other Plays. New York: Grove Press, Inc., 1977.

Every Good Boy Deserves Favor and *Professional Foul.* New York: Grove Press, Inc., 1978.

Dogg's Our Pet in *Ten of the Best British Short Plays,* ed. by Ed Berman. London: Inter-Action Inprint, 1979.

Dogg's Hamlet, Cahoot's Macbeth. London: Inter-Action Inprint, 1979.

Night and Day. New York: Grove Press, Inc., 1979.

Works About Tom Stoppard

Amory, Mark. "The Joke's the Thing." *Sunday Times Magazine* (June 9, 1974,) 64ff.

Ayer, A. J. "Love Among the Logical Positivists." *The Sunday Times* (April 9, 1972), 16.

Babula, William. "The Play-Life Metaphor in Shakespeare and Stoppard." *Modern Drama* 15 (1972), 279–281.

Bennett, Jonathan. "Philosophy and Mr Stoppard." *Philosophy* 50 (1975), 5–18.

Berlin, Normand. "*Rosencrantz and Guildenstern Are Dead:* Theatre of Criticism." *Modern Drama* (December 1973), 269–277.

Bigsby, C.W.E. *Tom Stoppard.* Burnt Mill, Harlow, Essex: Longman Group Ltd., 1976.

Cahn, Victor. *Beyond Absurdity: The Plays of Tom Stoppard* New Jersey: Fairleigh Dickinson University Press, 1979.

Crossley, Brian M. "An Investigation of Stoppard's 'Hound' and 'Foot'." *Modern Drama* (March 1977), 77–86.

Daniell, D.J. "Forward with Stoppard." *Theatre News* (May 1979), 20–21.

Gabbard, Lucina P. "Stoppard's *Jumpers:* A Mystery Play." *Modern Drama* (March 1977), 87–95.

Gianakaris, C.J. "Absurdism Altered: *Rosencrantz and Guildenstern Are Dead.*" *Drama Survey* (Winter 1968–69), 52–58.

Gitzen, Julian. "Tom Stoppard: Chaos in Perspective." *Southern Humanities Review* (1976), 143–152.

Gussow, Mel. "Schnitzler's Vienna as Told to Stoppard." *New York Times* (July 15, 1979), II, 6.

Hayman, Ronald. *Tom Stoppard.* London: Heinemann, 1978.

James, Clive. "Count Zero Splits the Infinite." *Encounter* (November 1975), 68–76.

Jensen, Henning. "Jonathan Bennett and Mr Stoppard." *Philosophy* 52 (1977), 214–217.

Kerr, Walter. "Tom Stoppard is Too Lazy to be Really Funny." *New York Times* (January 23, 1977), II, 3.

Keyssar-Franke, Helene. "The Strategy of *Rosencrantz and Guildenstern Are Dead.*" *Educational Theatre Journal* (March 1975), 85–97.

Lee, R.H. "The Circle and Its Tangent." *Theoria* (1969), 37–43.

Leonard, John. "Tom Stoppard Tries on a 'Knickers Farce'." *New York Times* (January 9, 1977), II, 1.

Levenson, Jill. "Views from a Revolving Door: Tom
    Stoppard's Canon to Date." *Queen's Quarterly* (Autumn
    1971), 431–442.

Robinson, Gabrielle Scott. "Plays Without Plot: The Theatre
    of Tom Stoppard." *Educational Theatre Journal* (March
    1977), 37–43.

Rosenwald, Peter J. "The Meaning of Nonsense." *Horizon*
    (November 1979) 38–43.

Ryan, Randolph. "Theatre Checklist No. 2: Tom Stoppard."
    Theatrefacts (May–July 1974), 3–9.

Shulman, Milton. "The Politicizing of Tom Stoppard." *New
    York Times* (April 23, 1978), 3, 27.

Stoppard, Tom. "Ambushes for the Audience: Towards a
    High Comedy of Ideas." *Theatre Quarterly* (May–July
    1974), 3–17.

Taylor, John Russell. "Tom Stoppard" in *The Second Wave;
    British Drama for the Seventies.* New York: Hill and
    Wang, 1971.

Tynan, Kenneth. "Profiles." *New Yorker* (December 19,
    1977), 41–111.

Weightman, John. "A Metaphysical Comedy." *Encounter*
    (April 1972), 44–46.

INDEX

MODERN LITERATURE SERIES
In the same series (continued from page ii)